Nginx Essentials

Excel in Nginx quickly by learning to use its most
essential features in real-life applications

Valery Kholodkov

BIRMINGHAM - MUMBAI

Nginx Essentials

First published: July 2015

Production reference: 1170715

Published by Packt Publishing Ltd.
Livery Place
35 Livery Street
Birmingham B3 2PB, UK.

ISBN 978-1-78528-953-8

www.packtpub.com

Credits

Author
Valery Kholodkov

Reviewers
Markus Jelsma

Jesse Estill Lawson

Daniel Parraz

Commissioning Editor
Dipika Gaonkar

Acquisition Editor
Usha Iyer

Content Development Editor
Nikhil Potdukhe

Technical Editor
Manali Gonsalves

Copy Editor
Roshni Banerjee

Project Coordinator
Vijay Kushlani

Proofreader
Safis Editing

Indexer
Priya Sane

Production Coordinator
Shantanu N. Zagade

Cover Work
Shantanu N. Zagade

About the Author

Valery Kholodkov is a seasoned IT professional with a decade of experience in creating, building, scaling, and maintaining industrial-grade web services, web applications, and mobile application backends. Throughout his career, he has worked for well-known brands, such as Yandex, Booking.com, and AVG. He currently works for his own consultancy firm. Valery has a deep understanding of technology and is able to express its essence, advantages, and risks to a layman, which makes him an accomplished author of technology books.

About the Reviewers

Markus Jelsma is CTO and co-owner at Openindex B.V., a Dutch company specializing in open source search and crawl solutions. As a committer and PMC member of Apache Nutch, he's an expert in search engine technology and web crawl solutions.

Jesse Estill Lawson is a computer scientist and social science researcher who works in higher education. He has consulted with dozens of colleges across the country to help them design, develop, and deploy computer information systems on everything from Windows and Apache to Nginx and node servers, and he centers his research on the coexistence of data science and sociology. In addition to his technological background, Jesse holds an MA in English and is currently working on his PhD in education. You can learn more about him on his website at http://lawsonry.com.

Daniel Parraz is a Linux systems administrator with 15 years of experience in high-volume e-retailer sites, large system storage, and security enterprises. He is currently working with a managed services provider, where he is responsible for all aspects of Unix-like systems in the organization. Daniel was also a technical editor for *Learning Nagios 4*, *Packt Publishing*, and has co-written training material for the IBM DS8000 storage server.

> I would like to thank my family, friends, and mentors for their constant support through the years.

www.PacktPub.com

Support files, eBooks, discount offers, and more

For support files and downloads related to your book, please visit www.PacktPub.com.

Did you know that Packt offers eBook versions of every book published, with PDF and ePub files available? You can upgrade to the eBook version at www.PacktPub.com and as a print book customer, you are entitled to a discount on the eBook copy. Get in touch with us at service@packtpub.com for more details.

At www.PacktPub.com, you can also read a collection of free technical articles, sign up for a range of free newsletters and receive exclusive discounts and offers on Packt books and eBooks.

https://www2.packtpub.com/books/subscription/packtlib

Do you need instant solutions to your IT questions? PacktLib is Packt's online digital book library. Here, you can search, access, and read Packt's entire library of books.

Why subscribe?

- Fully searchable across every book published by Packt
- Copy and paste, print, and bookmark content
- On demand and accessible via a web browser

Free access for Packt account holders

If you have an account with Packt at www.PacktPub.com, you can use this to access PacktLib today and view 9 entirely free books. Simply use your login credentials for immediate access.

Table of Contents

Preface

2006 was an exciting year. The disappointment that surrounded the dot-com crash had pretty much been superseded by a renewed and more confident growth of Web 2.0 and inspired a search for technologies of a new age.

At that time, I was looking for a web server to power my projects that would do many things in a different way. After getting some experience in large-scale online projects, I knew that the popular LAMP stack was suboptimal and sometimes did not solve certain challenges, such as efficient uploads, geo-dependent rate limiting, and so on.

After trying and rejecting a number of options, I came to know about Nginx and immediately felt that my search was over. It is small yet powerful, with a clean code base, good extensibility, relevant set of features, and a number of architectural challenges solved. Nginx definitely stood out from the crowd!

I immediately got inspired and felt some affinity to this project. I tried participating in the Nginx community, learned, shared my knowledge, and contributed as much as I could.

With time, my knowledge of Nginx grew. I started to get consultancy requests and have been capable of addressing quite sophisticated cases. After some time, I realized that some of my knowledge might be worth sharing with everyone. That's how I started a blog at www.nginxguts.com.

A blog turned out to be an author-driven medium. A more reader-focused and more thorough medium was in demand, so I set aside some time to assemble my knowledge in the more solid form of a book. That's how the book you're holding in your hands right now came into existence.

What this book covers

Chapter 1, Getting Started with Nginx, gives you the most basic knowledge about Nginx, including how to carry out the very basic installation and get Nginx up and running quickly. A detailed explanation of the structure of the configuration file is given so that you know where exactly code snippets from the rest of the book apply.

Chapter 2, Managing Nginx, explains how to manage an operating Nginx instance(s).

Chapter 3, Proxying and Caching, explains how to turn Nginx into a powerful web proxy and cache.

Chapter 4, Rewrite Engine and Access Control, explains how to use the rewrite engine to manipulate URLs and secure your web resources.

Chapter 5, Managing Inbound and Outbound Traffic, describes how to apply various restrictions to inbound traffic, and how to use and manage upstream.

Chapter 6, Performance Tuning, explains how to squeeze the most out of your Nginx server.

What you need for this book

A good knowledge of Unix-like operating systems is required, presumably Linux, along with some web master experience.

Who this book is for

This book intends to enrich web masters' and site reliability engineers' knowledge of subtleties known to those who have a deep understanding of the Nginx core. At the same time, this book is a *from the start* guide that allows beginners to easily switch to Nginx under experienced guidance.

Conventions

In this book, you will find a number of text styles that distinguish between different kinds of information. Here are some examples of these styles and an explanation of their meaning.

Code words in text, folder names, filenames, file extensions, pathnames, dummy URLs, and user input, are shown as follows: "We can include other contexts through the use of the `include` directive."

A block of code is set as follows:

```
types {
    text/html                   html htm shtml;
    text/css                    css;
    text/xml                    xml;
    image/gif                   gif;
    image/jpeg                  jpeg jpg;
    application/x-javascript    js;
    application/atom+xml        atom;
    application/rss+xml         rss;
}
```

When we wish to draw your attention to a particular part of a code block, the relevant lines or items are set in bold:

```
types {
    text/html                   html htm shtml;
    text/css                    css;
    text/xml                    xml;
    image/gif                   gif;
    image/jpeg                  jpeg jpg;
    application/x-javascript    js;
    application/atom+xml        atom;
    application/rss+xml         rss;
}
```

Any command-line input or output is written as follows:

```
# cp /usr/local/nginx/nginx.conf.default
    /etc/nginx/nginx.conf
```

New terms and **important words** are shown in bold. Words that you see on the screen, for example, in menus or dialog boxes, appear in the text like this: "Clicking the **Next** button moves you to the next screen."

 Warnings or important notes appear in a box like this.

 Tips and tricks appear like this.

Elisions of sections of configuration files are shown as [...] or with a comment [... this part of the configuration file is up to you ...]

Reader feedback

Feedback from our readers is always welcome. Let us know what you think about this book—what you liked or disliked. Reader feedback is important for us as it helps us develop titles that you will really get the most out of.

To send us general feedback, simply e-mail feedback@packtpub.com, and mention the book's title in the subject of your message.

If there is a topic that you have expertise in and you are interested in either writing or contributing to a book, see our author guide at www.packtpub.com/authors.

Customer support

Now that you are the proud owner of a Packt book, we have a number of things to help you to get the most from your purchase.

Errata

Although we have taken every care to ensure the accuracy of our content, mistakes do happen. If you find a mistake in one of our books—maybe a mistake in the text or the code—we would be grateful if you could report this to us. By doing so, you can save other readers from frustration and help us improve subsequent versions of this book. If you find any errata, please report them by visiting http://www.packtpub.com/submit-errata, selecting your book, clicking on the **Errata Submission Form** link, and entering the details of your errata. Once your errata are verified, your submission will be accepted and the errata will be uploaded to our website or added to any list of existing errata under the Errata section of that title.

To view the previously submitted errata, go to https://www.packtpub.com/books/content/support and enter the name of the book in the search field. The required information will appear under the **Errata** section.

Piracy

Piracy of copyrighted material on the Internet is an ongoing problem across all media. At Packt, we take the protection of our copyright and licenses very seriously. If you come across any illegal copies of our works in any form on the Internet, please provide us with the location address or website name immediately so that we can pursue a remedy.

Please contact us at copyright@packtpub.com with a link to the suspected pirated material.

We appreciate your help in protecting our authors and our ability to bring you valuable content.

eBooks, discount offers, and more

Did you know that Packt offers eBook versions of every book published, with PDF and ePub files available? You can upgrade to the eBook version at www.PacktPub.com and as a print book customer, you are entitled to a discount on the eBook copy. Get in touch with us at customercare@packtpub.com for more details.

At www.PacktPub.com, you can also read a collection of free technical articles, sign up for a range of free newsletters, and receive exclusive discounts and offers on Packt books and eBooks.

Questions

If you have a problem with any aspect of this book, you can contact us at questions@packtpub.com, and we will do our best to address the problem.

1
Getting Started with Nginx

Nginx has emerged as a robust and scalable general-purpose web server in the last decade. It is a choice of many webmasters, startup founders, and site reliability engineers because of its simple yet scalable and expandable architecture, easy configuration, and light memory footprint. Nginx offers a lot of useful features, such as on-the-fly compression and caching out of the box.

Nginx integrates with existing web technologies such as Apache web server and PHP, and helps solving day-to-day problems in an easy way. Nginx is backed by a large, active community as well as a consulting company funded by venture capital. Therefore, it is actively supported.

This book will help you get started with Nginx and learn skills necessary to turn it into a powerful tool, a workhorse that will help you to solve your day-to-day challenges.

Installing Nginx

Before you can dive into specific features of Nginx, you need to learn how to install Nginx on your system.

It is strongly recommended that you use prebuilt binary packages of Nginx if they are available in your distribution. This ensures best integration of Nginx with your system and reuse of best practices incorporated into the package by the package maintainer. Prebuilt binary packages of Nginx automatically maintain dependencies for you and package maintainers are usually fast to include security patches, so you don't get any complaints from security officers. In addition to that, the package usually provides a distribution-specific startup script, which doesn't come out of the box.

Refer to your distribution package directory to find out if you have a prebuilt package for Nginx. Prebuilt Nginx packages can also be found under the **download** link on the official Nginx.org site.

In this chapter, we will quickly go through most common distributions that contain prebuilt packages for Nginx.

Installing Nginx on Ubuntu

The Ubuntu Linux distribution contains a prebuilt package for Nginx. To install it, simply run the following command:

```
$ sudo apt-get install nginx
```

The preceding command will install all the required files on your system, including the `logrotate` script and service autorun scripts. The following table describes the Nginx installation layout that will be created after running this command as well as the purpose of the selected files and folders:

Description	Path/Folder
Nginx configuration files	`/etc/nginx`
Main configuration file	`/etc/nginx/nginx.conf`
Virtual hosts configuration files (including default one)	`/etc/nginx/sites-enabled`
Custom configuration files	`/etc/nginx/conf.d`
Log files (both access and error log)	`/var/log/nginx`
Temporary files	`/var/lib/nginx`
Default virtual host files	`/usr/share/nginx/html`

Default virtual host files will be placed into `/usr/share/nginx/html`. Please keep in mind that this directory is only for the default virtual host. For deploying your web application, use folders recommended by **Filesystem Hierarchy Standard** (**FHS**).

Now you can start the Nginx service with the following command:

```
$ sudo service nginx start
```

This will start Nginx on your system.

Alternatives

The prebuilt Nginx package on Ubuntu has a number of alternatives. Each of them allows you to fine tune the Nginx installation for your system.

Installing Nginx on Red Hat Enterprise Linux or CentOS/Scientific Linux

Nginx is not provided out of the box in Red Hat Enterprise Linux or CentOS/Scientific Linux. Instead, we will use the **Extra Packages for Enterprise Linux** (**EPEL**) repository. EPEL is a repository that is maintained by Red Hat Enterprise Linux maintainers, but contains packages that are not a part of the main distribution for various reasons. You can read more about EPEL at `https://fedoraproject.org/wiki/EPEL`.

To enable EPEL, you need to download and install the repository configuration package:

- For RHEL or CentOS/SL 7, use the following link:

  `http://download.fedoraproject.org/pub/epel/7/x86_64/repoview/epel-release.html`

- For RHEL/CentOS/SL 6 use the following link:

  `http://download.fedoraproject.org/pub/epel/6/i386/repoview/epel-release.html`

- If you have a newer/older RHEL version, please take a look at the *How can I use these extra packages?* section in the original EPEL wiki at the following link:

  `https://fedoraproject.org/wiki/EPEL`

Now that you are ready to install Nginx, use the following command:

```
# yum install nginx
```

The preceding command will install all the required files on your system, including the `logrotate` script and service autorun scripts. The following table describes the Nginx installation layout that will be created after running this command and the purpose of the selected files and folders:

Description	Path/Folder
Nginx configuration files	`/etc/nginx`
Main configuration file	`/etc/nginx/nginx.conf`
Virtual hosts configuration files (including default one)	`/etc/nginx/conf.d`
Custom configuration files	`/etc/nginx/conf.d`
Log files (both access and error log)	`/var/log/nginx`
Temporary files	`/var/lib/nginx`
Default virtual host files	`/usr/share/nginx/html`

Default virtual host files will be placed into `/usr/share/nginx/html`. Please keep in mind that this directory is only for the default virtual host. For deploying your web application, use folders recommended by FHS.

By default, the Nginx service will not autostart on system startup, so let's enable it. Refer to the following table for the commands corresponding to your CentOS version:

Function	Cent OS 6	Cent OS 7
Enable Nginx startup at system startup	`chkconfig nginx on`	`systemctl enable nginx`
Manually start Nginx	`service nginx start`	`systemctl start nginx`
Manually stop Nginx	`service nginx stop`	`systemctl start nginx`

Installing Nginx from source files

Traditionally, Nginx is distributed in the source code. In order to install Nginx from the source code, you need to download and compile the source files on your system.

It is not recommended that you install Nginx from the source code. Do this only if you have a good reason, such as the following scenarios:

- You are a software developer and want to debug or extend Nginx
- You feel confident enough to maintain your own package
- A package from your distribution is not good enough for you
- You want to fine-tune your Nginx binary

In either case, if you are planning to use this way of installing for real use, be prepared to sort out challenges such as dependency maintenance, distribution, and application of security patches.

In this section, we will be referring to the configuration script. Configuration script is a shell script similar to one generated by autoconf, which is required to properly configure the Nginx source code before it can be compiled. This configuration script has nothing to do with the Nginx configuration file that we will be discussing later.

Downloading the Nginx source files

The primary source for Nginx for an English-speaking audience is Nginx.org. Open http://nginx.org/en/download.html in your browser and choose the most recent stable version of Nginx. Download the chosen archive into a directory of your choice (/usr/local or /usr/src are common directories to use for compiling software):

```
$ wget -q http://nginx.org/download/nginx-1.7.9.tar.gz
```

Extract the files from the downloaded archive and change to the directory corresponding to the chosen version of Nginx:

```
$ tar xf nginx-1.7.9.tar.gz
$ cd nginx-1.7.9
```

To configure the source code, we need to run the ./configure script included in the archive:

```
$ ./configure
checking for OS
 + Linux 3.13.0-36-generic i686
checking for C compiler ... found
+ using GNU C compiler
[...]
```

This script will produce a lot of output and, if successful, will generate a Makefile file for the source files.

Notice that we showed the non-privileged user prompt $ instead of the root # in the previous command lines. You are encouraged to configure and compile software as a regular user and only install as root. This will prevent a lot of problems related to access restriction while working with the source code.

Troubleshooting

The troubleshooting step, although very simple, has a couple of common pitfalls. The basic installation of Nginx requires the presence of OpenSSL and **Perl-compatible Regex (PCRE)** developer packages in order to compile. If these packages are not properly installed or not installed in locations where the Nginx configuration script is able to locate them, the configuration step might fail.

Then, you have to choose between disabling the affected Nginx built-in modules (rewrite or SSL, installing required packages properly, or pointing the Nginx configuration script to the actual location of those packages if they are installed.

Building Nginx

You can build the source files now using the following command:

```
$ make
```

You'll see a lot of output on compilation. If build is successful, you can install the Nginx file on your system. Before doing that, make sure you escalate your privileges to the super user so that the installation script can install the necessary files into the system areas and assign necessary privileges. Once successful, run the `make install` command:

```
# make install
```

The preceding command will install all the necessary files on your system. The following table lists all locations of the Nginx files that will be created after running this command and their purposes:

Description	Path/Folder
Nginx configuration files	`/usr/local/nginx/conf`
Main configuration file	`/usr/local/nginx/conf/nginx.conf`
Log files (both access and error log)	`/usr/local/nginx/logs`
Temporary files	`/usr/local/nginx`
Default virtual host files	`/usr/local/nginx/html`

 Unlike installations from prebuilt packages, installation from source files does not harness Nginx folders for the custom configuration files or virtual host configuration files. The main configuration file is also very simple in its nature. You have to take care of this yourself.

Nginx must be ready to use now. To start Nginx, change your working directory to the `/usr/local/nginx` directory and run the following command:

```
# sbin/nginx
```

This will start Nginx on your system with the default configuration.

Troubleshooting

This stage works flawlessly most of the time. A problem can occur in the following situations:

- You are using nonstandard system configuration. Try to play with the options in the configuration script in order to overcome the problem.

- You compiled in third-party modules and they are out of date or not maintained.

Switch off third-party modules that break your build or contact the developer for assistance.

Copying the source code configuration from prebuilt packages

Occasionally you might want to amend Nginx binary from a prebuilt packages with your own changes. In order to do that you need to reproduce the build tree that was used to compile Nginx binary for the prebuilt package.

But how would you know what version of Nginx and what configuration script options were used at the build time? Fortunately, Nginx has a solution for that. Just run the existing Nginx binary with the -V command-line option. Nginx will print the configure-time options. This is shown in the following:

```
$ /usr/sbin/nginx -V
nginx version: nginx/1.4.6 (Ubuntu)
built by gcc 4.8.2 (Ubuntu 4.8.2-19ubuntu1)
TLS SNI support enabled
configure arguments: --with-cc-opt='-g -O2 -fstack-protector --param=ssp-
buffer-size=4 -Wformat -Werror=format-security -D_FORTIFY_SOURCE=2'
--with-ld-opt='-Wl,-Bsymbolic-functions -Wl,-z,relro' ...
```

Using the output of the preceding command, reproduce the entire build environment, including the Nginx source tree of the corresponding version and modules that were included into the build.

Here, the output of the Nginx -V command is trimmed for simplicity. In reality, you will be able to see and copy the entire command line that was passed to the configuration script at the build time.

You might even want to reproduce the version of the compiler used in order to produce a binary-identical Nginx executable file (we will discuss this later when discussing how to troubleshoot crashes).

Once this is done, run the ./configure script of your Nginx source tree with options from the output of the -V option (with necessary alterations) and follow the remaining steps of the build procedure. You will get an altered Nginx executable on the objs/ folder of the source tree.

The structure of the Nginx installation

When Nginx is installed, we can quickly study the structure of the installation. This will help you to know your installation better and manage it more confidently.

For each installation method, we have a set of generic locations and default paths. Let's see what these default locations contain.

The Nginx configuration folder

This folder contains the main configuration file and a set of parameter files. The following table describes the purpose of each of the default parameter files:

File name	Description
mime.types	This contains the default MIME type map for converting file extensions into MIME types.
fastcgi_params	This contains the default FastCGI parameters required for FastCGI to function.
scgi_params	This contains the default SCGI parameters required for SCGI to function.
uwsgi_params	This contains the default UWCGI parameters required for UWCGI to function.
proxy_params	This contains the default proxy module parameters. This parameter set is required for certain web servers when they are behind Nginx, so that they can figure out they are behind a proxy.
naxsi.rules (optional)	This is the main rule set for the NAXSI web application firewall module.
koi-utf, koi-win, and win-utf	These are the Cyrillic character set conversion tables.

The default virtual host folder

The default configuration contains references to this site as root. It is not recommended that you use this directory for real sites, as it is not a good practice for the Nginx folders hierarchy to contain the site hierarchy. Use this directory for testing purposes or for serving auxiliary files.

The virtual hosts configuration folder

This is the location of virtual host configuration files. The recommended structure of this folder is to have one file per virtual host in this folder or one folder per virtual host, containing all files related to this virtual host. In this way, you will always know which files were used and which are now being used, and what each of the files contain and which files can be purged.

The log folder

This is the location for Nginx log files. The default access log file and error log file will be written to this location. For installation from source files, it is not recommended that you use the default location `/usr/local/nginx/logs` for real sites. Instead, make sure all your log files are stored in the system log file location, such as `/var/log/nginx`, to provide better overview and management of your log files.

The temporary folder

Nginx uses temporary files for receiving large request bodies, and proxies large files from upstream. Files that are created for this purpose can be found in this folder.

Configuring Nginx

Now that you know how to install Nginx and the structure of its installation, we can study how to configure Nginx. Simplicity of configuration is one of the reasons Nginx is popular among webmasters, because this saves them a lot of time.

In a nutshell, Nginx configuration files are simply sequences of directives that can take up to eight space-separated arguments, for example:

```
gzip_types text/plain text/css application/x-javascript text/xml
application/xml application/xml+rss text/javascript;
```

In the configuration file, the directives are delimited by a semicolon (;) from one another. Some of the directives may have a block instead of a semicolon. A block is delimited by curly brackets ({}). A block can contain arbitrary text data, for example:

```
types {
    text/html                      html htm shtml;
    text/css                          css;
    text/xml                          xml;
    image/gif                         gif;
```

```
      image/jpeg                          jpeg jpg;
      application/x-javascript      js;
      application/atom+xml          atom;
      application/rss+xml            rss;
}
```

A block can also contain a list of other directives. In this case, the block is called a section. A section can enclose other sections, thus establishing a hierarchy of sections.

Most important directives have short names; this reduces the effort required to maintain the configuration file.

Value types

In general, a directive can have arbitrary quoted or unquoted strings as arguments. But many directives have arguments that have common value types. To help you quickly get your head around the value types I listed them in the following table:

Value type	Format	Example of a value
Flag	[on	off]	on, off
Signed integer	-?[0-9]+	1024
Size	[0-9]+([mM] | [kK])?	23M, 12348k
Offset	[0-9]+([mM] | [kK] | [gG])?	43G, 256M
Milliseconds	[0-9]+[yMwdhms]?	30s, 60m

Variables

Variables are named objects that can be assigned a textual value. Variables can only appear inside the http section. A variable is referred to by its name, prefixed by the dollar ($) symbol. Alternatively, a variable reference can enclose a variable name in curly brackets to prevent merging with surrounding text.

Variables can be used in any directive that accepts them, as shown here:

```
proxy_set_header Host $http_host;
```

This directive sets the HTTP header host in a forwarded request to HTTP host name from the original request. This is equivalent to the following:

```
proxy_set_header Host ${http_host};
```

With the following syntax, you can specify the host name:

```
proxy_set_header Host ${http_host}_squirrel;
```

The preceding command will append a string `_squirrel` to the value of the original host name. Without curly brackets, the string `_squirrel` would have been interpreted as a part of the variable name, and the reference would have pointed to a variable "http_host_squirrel" rather than `http_host`.

There are also special variable names:

- Variables from `$1` to `$9` refer to the capture arguments in the regular expressions, as shown here:

```
location ~ /(.+)\.php$ {
    [...]
    proxy_set_header X-Script-Name $1;
}
```

  The preceding configuration will set the HTTP header `X-Script-Name` in the forwarded request to the name of the PHP script in the request URI. The captures are specified in a regular expression using round brackets.

- Variables that start with `$arg_` refer to the corresponding query argument in the original HTTP request, as shown here:

```
proxy_set_header X-Version-Name $arg_ver;
```

  The preceding configuration will set the HTTP header `X-Version-Name` in the forwarded request to the value of the `ver` query argument in the original request.

- Variables that start with `$http_` refer to the corresponding HTTP header line in the original request.

- Variables that start with `$sent_http_` refer to the corresponding HTTP header line in the outbound HTTP request.

- Variables that start with `$upstream_http_` refer to the corresponding HTTP header line in the response received from an upstream.

- Variables that start with `$cookie_` refer to the corresponding cookie in the original request.

- Variables that start with `$upstream_cookie_` refer to the corresponding cookie in the response received from an upstream.

Variables must be declared by Nginx modules before they can be used in the configuration. Built-in Nginx modules provide a set of core variables that allow you to operate with the data from HTTP requests and responses. Refer to the Nginx documentation for the complete list of core variables and their functions.

Third-party modules can provide extra variables. These variables have to be described in the third-party module's documentation.

Inclusions

Any Nginx configuration section can contain inclusions of other files via the `include` directive. This directive takes a single argument containing a path to a file to be included, as shown here:

```
/*
 * A simple relative inclusion. The target file's path
 * is relative to the location of the current configuration file.
 */
include mime.types;

/*
 * A simple inclusion using an absolute path.
 */
include /etc/nginx/conf/site-defaults.conf;
```

Once specified, the `include` directive instructs Nginx to process the contents of the file or files specified by the argument of this directive as if they were specified in place of the `include` directive.

 Relative paths are resolved with respect to the path of the configuration file the directive is specified in. This is good to keep in mind when the `include` directive is specified in another included file, such as when a virtual host configuration file contains a relative `include` directive.

The `include` directive can also contain a globbed path with wild cards, either relative or absolute. In this case, the globbed path is expanded and all files matching the specified pattern are included in no particular order. Take a look at the following code:

```
/*
 * A simple glob inclusion. This will include all files
 * ending on ".conf" located in /etc/nginx/sites-enabled
 */
include /etc/nginx/sites-enabled/*.conf;
```

The `include` directive with wild cards is an obvious solution for including site configurations, as their number can vary greatly. Using the `include` directive, you can properly structure the configuration file or reuse certain parts multiple times.

Sections

A section is a directive that encloses other directives in its block. Each section's delimiters must be located in the same file, while the content of a section can span multiple files via the `include` directive.

It is not possible to describe every possible configuration directive in this chapter. Refer to the Nginx documentation for more information. However, I will quickly go over the Nginx configuration section types so that you can orient in the structure of the Nginx configuration files.

The http section

The `http` section enables and configures the HTTP service in Nginx. It has the server and upstream declarations. As far as individual directives are concerned, the `http` section usually contains those that specify defaults for the entire HTTP service.

The `http` section must contain at least one `server` section in order to process HTTP requests. Here is a typical layout of the `http` section:

```
http {
    [...]
    server {
        [...]
    }
}
```

Here and in other examples of this book, we use [...] to refer to omitted irrelevant parts of the configuration.

The server section

The `server` section configures an HTTP or HTTPS virtual host and specifies listening addresses for them using the `listen` directive. At the end of the configuration stage, all listening addresses are grouped together and all listening addresses are activated at startup.

The `server` section contains the `location` sections, as well as sections that can be enclosed by the `location` section (see description of other sections types for details). Directives that are specified in the `server` section itself go into the so-called default location. In that regard, the `server` section serves the purpose of the `location` section itself.

When a request comes in via one of the listening addresses, it is routed to the server sections that match a virtual host pattern specified by the server_name directive. The request is then routed further to the location that matches the path of the request URI or processed by the default location if there is no match.

The upstream section

The upstream section configures a logical server that Nginx can pass requests to for further processing. This logical server can be configured to be backed by one or more physical servers external to Nginx with concrete domain names or IP addresses.

Upstream can be referred to by name from any place in the configuration file where a reference to a physical server can take place. In this way, your configuration can be made independent of the underlying structure of the upstream, while the upstream structure can be changed without changing your configuration.

The location section

The location section is one of the workhorses in Nginx. The location directive takes parameters that specify a pattern that is matched against the path of the request URI. When a request is routed to a location, Nginx activates configuration that is enclosed by that location section.

There are three types of location patterns: simple, exact, and regular expression location patterns.

Simple

A simple location has a string as the first argument. When this string matches the initial part of the request URI, the request is routed to that location. Here is an example of a simple location:

```
location /images {
    root /usr/local/html/images;
}
```

Any request with a URI that starts with /images, such as /images/powerlogo.png, /images/calendar.png, or /images/social/github-icon.png will be routed to this location. A URI with a path that equals to /images will be routed to this location as well.

Exact

Exact locations are designated with an equals (=) character as the first argument and have a string as the second argument, just like simple locations do. Essentially, exact locations work just like simple locations, except that the path in the request URI has to match the second argument of the `location` directive exactly in order to be routed to that location:

```
location = /images/empty.gif {
    emptygif;
}
```

The preceding configuration will return an empty GIF file if and only if the URI `/images/empty.gif` is requested.

Regular expression locations

Regular expression locations are designated with a tilde (~) character or ~*
(for case-insensitive matches) as the first argument and have a regular expression as the second argument. Regular expression locations are processed after both simple and exact locations. The path in the request URI has to match the regular expression in the second argument of the `location` directive in order to be routed to that location. A typical example is as follows:

```
location ~ \.php$ {
    [...]
}
```

According to the preceding configuration, requests with URIs that end with `.php` will be routed to this location.

The `location` sections can be nested. For that, you just need to specify a `location` section inside another `location` section.

The if section

The `if` section encloses a configuration that becomes active once a condition specified by the `if` directive is satisfied. The `if` section can be enclosed by the `server` and `location` sections, and is only available if the `rewrite` module is present.

A condition of an `if` directive is specified in round brackets and can take the following forms:

- A plain variable, as shown here:

```
if ($file_present) {
    limit_rate 256k;
}
```

If the variable evaluates to true value in runtime, the configuration section activates.

- A unary expression that consists of an operator and a string with variables, as shown here:

```
if ( -d "${path}" ) {
    try_files "${path}/default.png" "${path}/default.jpg";
}
```

The following unary operators are supported:

Operator	Description	Operator	Description
-f	True if specified file exists	!-f	True if specified file does not exist
-d	True if specified directory exists	!-d	True if specified directory does not exist
-e	True if specified file exists and is a symbolic link	!-e	True if specified file does not exist or is not a symbolic link
-x	True if specified file exists and is executable	!-x	True if specified file does not exist or is not executable

- A binary expression that consists of a variable name, an operator, and a string with variables. The following binary operators are supported:

Operator	Description	Operator	Description
=	True if a variable matches a string	!=	True if a variable does not match a string
~	True if a regular expression matches the value of a variable	!~	True if a regular expression does not match the value of a variable
~*	True if a case-insensitive regular expression matches the value of a variable	!~*	True if a case-insensitive regular expression does not match the value of a variable

Let's discuss some examples of the `if` directive.

This one adds a prefix /msie/ to the URL of any request that contains MSIE in the user-agent field:

```
if ($http_user_agent ~ MSIE) {
    rewrite ^(.*)$ /msie/$1 break;
}
```

The next example sets the variable $id to the value of the cookie named id, if it is present:

```
if ($http_cookie ~* "id=([^;]+)(?:;|$)") {
    set $id $1;
}
```

The next one returns HTTP status 405 ("Method Not Allowed") for every request with the method POST:

```
if ($request_method = POST) {
    return 405;
}
```

Finally, the configuration in the following example limits the rate to 10 KB whenever the variable $slow evaluates to true:

```
if ($slow) {
    limit_rate 10k;
}
```

The if directive seems like a powerful instrument, but it must be used with caution. This is because the configuration inside the if section is not imperative, that is, it does not alter the request processing flow according to the order of the if directives.

 Because of the nonintuitive behavior of the if directive, its use is discouraged.

Conditions are not evaluated in the order they are specified in the configuration file. They are merely applied simultaneously and configuration settings from the sections for which conditions were satisfied are merged together and applied at once.

The limit_except section

The limit_except section activates the configuration that it encloses if the request method *does not match* any from the list of methods specified by this directive. Specifying the GET method in the list of methods automatically assumes the HEAD method. This section can only appear inside the location section, as shown here:

```
limit_except GET {
    return 405;
}
```

The preceding configuration will respond with HTTP status 405 ("Method Not Allowed") for every request that is not made using the GET or HEAD method.

Other section types

Nginx configuration can contain other section types, such as main and server in the main section, as well as section types provided by third-party modules. In this book, we will not pay close attention to them.

Refer to the documentation of the corresponding modules for information about these types of configuration sections.

Configuration settings' inheritance rules

Many Nginx configuration settings can be inherited from a section of outer level to a section of inner level. This saves a lot of time when you configure Nginx.

The following figure illustrates how inheritance rules work:

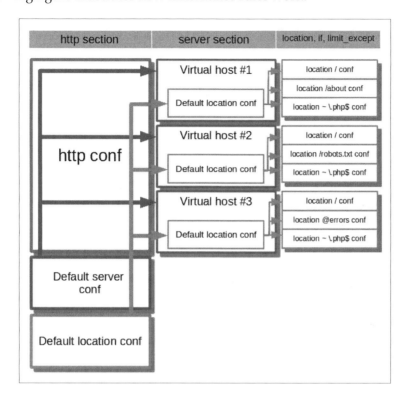

All settings can be attributed to three categories:

- Those that make sense only in the entire HTTP service (marked red)
- Those that make sense in the virtual host configuration (marked blue)
- Those that make sense on all levels of configuration (marked green)

The settings from the first category do not have any inheritance rules, because they cannot inherit values from anywhere. They can be specified in the http section only and can be applied to the entire HTTP service. These are settings set by directives, such as `variables_hash_max_size`, `variables_hash_bucket_size`, `server_names_hash_max_size`, and `server_names_hash_bucket_size`.

The settings from the second category can inherit values only from the http section. They can be specified both in the http and server sections, but the settings applied to a given virtual host are determined by inheritance rules. These are settings set by directives, such as `client_header_timeout`, `client_header_buffer_size`, and `large_client_header_buffers`.

Finally, the settings from the third category can inherit values from any section up to `http`. They can be specified in any section inside the HTTP service configuration, and the settings applied to a given context are determined by inheritance rules.

The arrows on the figure illustrate value propagation paths. The colors of the arrows specify the scope of the setting. The propagation rules along a path are as follows:

When you specify a value for a parameter at a certain level of the configuration, it overrides the value of the same parameter at the outer levels if it is set, and automatically propagates to the inner levels of the configuration. Let's take a look at the following example:

```
location / {
    # The outer section
    root /var/www/example.com;
    gzip on;

    location ~ \.js$ {
        # Inner section 1
        gzip off;

    }
    location ~ \.css$ {
        # Inner section 2
    }
    [...]
}
```

The value of the `root` directive will propagate to the inner sections, so there is no need to specify it again. The value of the `gzip` directive in the outer section will propagate to the inner sections, but will be overridden by the value of the `gzip` directive inside the first inner section. The overall effect of that will be that `gzip` compression will be enabled everywhere in the other section, except for the first inner section.

When a value for some parameter is not specified in a given configuration section, it is inherited from a section that encloses the current configuration section. If the enclosing section does not have this parameter set, the search goes to the outer level and so on. If a value for a certain parameter is not specified at all, a built-in default value is used.

The First sample configuration

By this point in the chapter, you might have accumulated a lot of knowledge without having an idea of what a complete working configuration looks like. We will study a short but functioning configuration that will give you an idea of what a complete configuration file might look like:

```
error_log logs/error.log;

events {
    use epoll;
    worker_connections  1024;
}

http {
    include          mime.types;
    default_type     application/octet-stream;

    server {
        listen      80;
        server_name example.org www.example.org;

        location / {
            proxy_pass http://localhost:8080;
            include proxy_params;
        }

        location ~ ^(/images|/js|/css) {
            root html;
            expires 30d;
        }
    }
}
```

This configuration first instructs Nginx to write the error log to `logs/error.log`. Then, it sets up Nginx to use the epoll event processing method (`use epoll`) and allocates memory for 1024 connections per worker (`worker_connections 1024`). After that, it enables the HTTP service and configures certain default settings for the HTTP service (`include mime.types`, `default_type application/octet-stream`). It creates a virtual host and sets its names to `example.org` and `www.example.org` (`server_name example.org www.example.org`). The virtual host is made available at the default listening address `0.0.0.0` and port 80 (`listen 80`).

We then configure two locations. The first location passes every request routed to it into a web application server running at `http://localhost:8080` (proxy_pass `http://localhost:8080`). The second location is a regular expression location. By specifying it we effectively exclude a set of paths from the first location. We use this location to return static data such as images, JavaScript files, and CSS files. We set the base directory for our media files as `html` (root html). For all media files, we set the expiration date as 30 days (`expires 30d`).

To try out this configuration, back up your default configuration file and replace the content of the default configuration file with the preceding configuration.

Then, restart Nginx for the settings to take effect. After this is done, you can navigate to the URL `http://localhost/` to check out your new configuration.

Configuration best practices

Now that you know more about the elements and structure of the Nginx configuration file, you might be curious about what best practices exist in this area. Here is a list of recommendations that will help you to maintain your configuration more efficiently and make it more robust and manageable:

- Structure your configuration well. Observe which common parts of the configuration are used more often, move them to separate files, and reuse them using the `include` directive. In addition to that, try to make each file in your configuration file hierarchy of a reasonable length, ideally no more than two screens. This will help you to read your files quicker and navigate over them efficiently.

> It is important to know exactly how your configuration works to successfully manage it. If the configuration doesn't work the way you expect, you might run into issues due to wrong settings being applied, for example, unavailability of arbitrary URIs, unexpected outages, and security loopholes.

- Minimize use of the `if` directive. The `if` directive has a nonintuitive behavior. Try to avoid using it whenever possible to make sure configuration settings are applied to the incoming requests as you expect.

- Use good defaults. Experiment with inheritance rules and try to come up with defaults for your settings so that they result in the least number of directives to be configured. This includes moving common settings from location to the server level and further to the HTTP level.

Summary

In this chapter, you learned how to install Nginx from a number of available sources, the structure of Nginx installation and the purpose of various files, the elements and structure of the Nginx configuration file, and how to create a minimal working Nginx configuration file. You also learned about some best practices for Nginx configuration.

In the next chapter, you will learn how to put Nginx into operation and how to manage it in action.

2
Managing Nginx

In a web server running at full scale, thousands of events are occurring each second. Micromanaging these events is obviously not possible, yet even small glitches are able to cause serious deterioration of quality of service and affect user experience.

To prevent theses glitches from happening, a dedicated webmaster or site reliability engineer must be able to understand and properly manage the processes behind the scenes.

In this chapter, you will learn how to manage an Nginx instance in operation, and we will discuss the following topics:

- Starting and stopping Nginx
- Reloading and reconfiguring processes
- Allocating worker processes
- Other management questions

The Nginx connection processing architecture

Before you study the management procedures of Nginx, you need to get some idea of how Nginx processes connections. In the full-scale mode, a single Nginx instance consists of the **master process** and **worker processes**, as shown in the following figure:

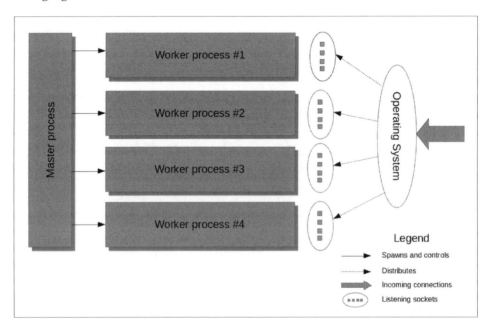

The master process spawns worker processes and controls them by sending and forwarding signals and listening for quit notifications from them. Worker processes wait on listening sockets and accept incoming connections. The operating system distributes incoming connections among worker processes in a round-robin fashion.

The master process is responsible for all startup, shutdown, and maintenance tasks such as the following:

- Reading and re-reading configuration files
- Opening and reopening log files
- Creating listening sockets
- Starting and restarting worker processes
- Forwarding signals to the worker processes
- Starting a new binary

The master process thus ensures continuous operation of an Nginx instance in the face of various changes in the environment and occasional crashes of worker processes.

Worker processes are responsible for serving connections and accepting new ones. Worker processes can run certain maintenance tasks as well. For instance, they reopen log files on their own after the master process has ensured that this operation is safe. Each worker process handles multiple connections. This is achieved by running an event loop that pulls events that occurred on open sockets from the operating system via a special system call, and quickly processing all pulled events by reading from and writing to active sockets. Resources required to maintain a connection are allocated when a worker process starts. The maximum number of connections that a worker process can handle simultaneously is configured by the worker_connections directive and defaults to 512.

In a **clustered setup**, a special routing device such as a load balancer or another Nginx instance is used to balance incoming connections among a set of identical Nginx instances, each of them consisting of a master process and a collection of worker processes. This is shown in the following figure:

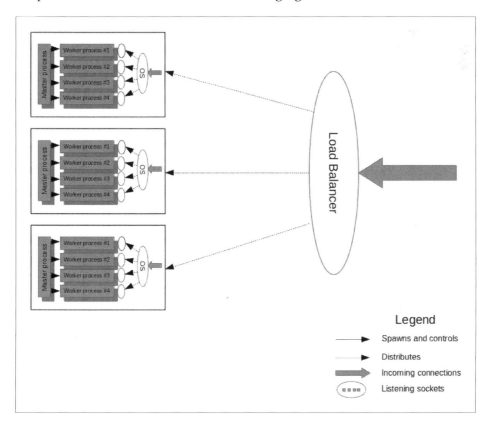

In this setup, the load balancer routes connections only to those instances that are listening for incoming connections. The load balancer ensures that each of the active instances gets an approximately equal amount of traffic, and routes traffic away from an instance if it shows any connectivity problems.

Because of the difference in the architecture, the management procedures for a clustered setup are slightly different than for a **standalone instance**. We will discuss these differences soon.

Starting and stopping Nginx

In the previous chapter, you learned a bit about how to start your Nginx instance. On Ubuntu, Debian, or Redhat-like systems you can run the following command:

```
# service nginx start
```

In the absence of startup scripts, you can simply run the binary using the following command:

```
# sbin/nginx
```

Nginx will read and parse the configuration file, create a PID file (a file containing its process ID), open log files, create listening sockets, and start worker processes. Once worker processes have started, a Nginx instance is able to respond to incoming connections. This is what a running Nginx instance looks like in the process list:

```
# ps -C nginx -f
UID          PID  PPID  C STIME TTY          TIME CMD
root        2324     1  0 15:30 ?        00:00:00 nginx: master process /
usr/sbin/nginx
www-data    2325  2324  0 15:30 ?        00:00:00 nginx: worker process
www-data    2326  2324  0 15:30 ?        00:00:00 nginx: worker process
www-data    2327  2324  0 15:30 ?        00:00:00 nginx: worker process
www-data    2328  2324  0 15:30 ?        00:00:00 nginx: worker process
```

Every Nginx process sets its process title such that it conveniently reflects the role of the process. Here, for example, you see the master process of the instance with process ID 2324 and four worker processes with process IDs 2325, 2326, 2327, and 2328. Note how the **parent process ID (PPID)** column points at the master process. We will refer to the ID of the master process further in this section.

If you can't find your instance in the process list or you see an error message on the console upon startup, something is preventing Nginx from starting. The following table lists potential issues and their solutions:

Message	Issue	Resolution
`[emerg] bind() to x.x.x.x:x failed (98: Address already in use)`	Conflicting listening endpoint	Make sure endpoints specified by the `listen` directive do not conflict with other services
`[emerg] open() "<path to file>" failed (2: No such file or directory)`	Invalid path to a file	Make sure all paths in your configuration point to existing directories
`[emerg] open() "<path to file>" failed (13: Permission denied)`	Insufficient privileges	Make sure all paths in your configuration point to directories that Nginx has access to

To stop Nginx, you can run the following command if a startup script is available:

```
# service nginx stop
```

Alternatively, you can send the TERM or INT signal to the master process of your instance to trigger a fast shutdown or the QUIT signal to trigger a graceful shutdown, as shown here:

```
# kill -QUIT 2324
```

The preceding command will trigger the graceful shutdown procedure on the instance and all processes will eventually quit. Here, we refer to the process ID of the master process from the preceding process list.

Control signals and their usage

Nginx, like any other Unix background service, is controlled by signals. Signals are asynchronous events that interrupt normal execution of a process and activate certain functions. The following table lists all signals that Nginx supports and the functions that they trigger:

Signal	Function
TERM, INT	Fast shutdown
QUIT	Graceful shutdown
HUP	Reconfiguration
USR1	Log file reopening
USR2	Nginx binary upgrade
WINCH	Graceful worker shutdown

All signals must be sent to the master process of an instance. The master process of an instance can be located by looking it up in the process list:

```
# ps -C nginx -f
UID         PID  PPID  C STIME TTY          TIME CMD
root       4754  3201  0 11:10 ?        00:00:00 nginx: master process /
usr/sbin/nginx
www-data   4755  4754  0 11:10 ?        00:00:00 nginx: worker process
www-data   4756  4754  0 11:10 ?        00:00:00 nginx: worker process
www-data   4757  4754  0 11:10 ?        00:00:00 nginx: worker process
www-data   4758  4754  0 11:10 ?        00:00:00 nginx: worker process
```

In this listing, the master process has a process ID 4754 and four worker processes. The process ID of the master process can be also obtained by examining the content of the PID file:

```
# cat /var/run/nginx.pid
4754
```

 Note: The path of nginx.pid might vary in different systems. You can use the /usr/sbin/nginx -V command to find out the exact path.

To send a signal to an instance, use the kill command and specify the process ID of the master process as the last argument:

```
# kill -HUP 4754
```

Alternatively, you can use command substitution to take the process ID of the master process directly from the PID file:

```
# kill -HUP `cat /var/run/nginx.pid`
```

You can also use the following command:

```
# kill - HUP $(cat /var/run/nginx.pid)
```

The preceding three commands will trigger reconfiguration of the instance. We will now discuss each of the functions that signals trigger in Nginx.

Fast shutdown

The TERM and INT signals are sent to the master process of an Nginx instance to trigger the fast shutdown procedure. All resources such as connections, open files and log files that each worker process is in possession of are immediately closed. After that, each worker process quits and the master process gets notified. Once all worker processes quit, the master process quits and shutdown is completed.

A fast shutdown obviously causes visible service outage. Therefore, it must be used either in emergency situations or when you are absolutely sure that nobody is using your instance.

Graceful shutdown

Once Nginx receives the QUIT signal, it enters graceful shutdown mode. Nginx closes listening sockets and accepts no new connections from then on. Existing connections are still served until no longer needed. Therefore, graceful shutdown might take a long time to complete, especially if some of the connections are in the middle of a long download or upload.

After you have signaled graceful shutdown to Nginx, you can monitor your process list to see which Nginx worker processes are still running and keep track of the progress of your shutdown procedure:

```
# ps -C nginx -f
UID         PID  PPID  C STIME TTY          TIME CMD
root       5813  3201  0 12:07 ?        00:00:00 nginx: master process /
usr/sbin/nginx
www-data   5814  5813 11 12:07 ?        00:00:01 nginx: worker process is
shutting down
```

In this listing, you can see an instance after a graceful shutdown has been triggered. A single worker process has an is shutting down label and its process title is marking a process that is currently shutting down.

Once all connections handled by a worker are closed, the worker process quits and the master process gets notified. Once all worker processes quit, the master process quits and shutdown is completed.

In a clustered or load-balanced setup, graceful shutdown is a typical way of putting an instance out of operation. Using graceful shutdown ensures that there are no visible outages of your service due to server reconfiguration or maintenance.

In a single instance, graceful shutdown can only make sure that existing connections are not closed abruptly. Once graceful shutdown is triggered on a single instance, the service will immediately be unavailable for new visitors. To ensure continuous availability on a single instance, use maintenance procedures such as reconfiguration, log file reopening, and Nginx binary update.

Reconfiguration

The HUP signal can be used to signal Nginx to reread the configuration files and restart worker processes. This procedure cannot be performed without restarting worker processes, as configuration data structures cannot be changed while a worker process is running.

Once the master process receives the HUP signals, it tries to reread the configuration files. If the configuration files can be parsed and contain no errors, the master process signals all the existing worker process to gracefully shut down. After signaling, it starts new worker processes with the new configuration.

As with graceful shutdown, the reconfiguration procedure might take a long time to complete. After you have signaled the reconfiguration to Nginx, you can monitor your process list to see which old Nginx worker processes are still running and keep track of the progress of your reconfiguration.

If another reconfiguration is triggered during a running reconfiguration procedure, Nginx will start a new collection of worker processes — even though worker processes from the past two rounds have not finished. This, in principle, might lead to excessive process table usage, so it's recommended that you wait until the current reconfiguration procedure is finished before starting a new one.

Here is an example of a reconfiguration procedure:

```
# ps -C nginx -f
UID         PID  PPID  C STIME TTY        TIME CMD
root        5887 3201  0 12:14 ?      00:00:00 nginx: master process /
usr/sbin/nginx
www-data    5888 5887  0 12:14 ?      00:00:00 nginx: worker process
www-data    5889 5887  0 12:14 ?      00:00:00 nginx: worker process
www-data    5890 5887  0 12:14 ?      00:00:00 nginx: worker process
www-data    5891 5887  0 12:14 ?      00:00:00 nginx: worker process
```

This listing shows an operating Nginx instance. The master process has a process ID of 5887. Let's send an HUP signal to the master process of the instance:

```
# kill -HUP 5887
```

The instance will change in the following way:

```
# ps -C nginx -f
UID         PID  PPID  C STIME TTY        TIME CMD
root        5887 3201  0 12:14 ?      00:00:00 nginx: master process /
usr/sbin/nginx
www-data    5888 5887  5 12:14 ?      00:00:07 nginx: worker process is
shutting down
www-data    5889 5887  0 12:14 ?      00:00:01 nginx: worker process is
shutting down
www-data    5890 5887  0 12:14 ?      00:00:00 nginx: worker process is
shutting down
www-data    5891 5887  0 12:14 ?      00:00:00 nginx: worker process is
shutting down
www-data    5918 5887  0 12:16 ?      00:00:00 nginx: worker process
www-data    5919 5887  0 12:16 ?      00:00:00 nginx: worker process
www-data    5920 5887  0 12:16 ?      00:00:00 nginx: worker process
www-data    5921 5887  0 12:16 ?      00:00:00 nginx: worker process
```

As you can see, the old worker processes with process IDs 5888, 5889, 5890, and 5891 are currently shutting down. The master process has re-read the configuration files and spawned a new collection of worker processes with process IDs 5918, 5919, 5920, and 5921.

After a while, old worker processes will terminate and the instance will look like it did before:

```
# ps -C nginx -f
UID          PID  PPID  C STIME TTY          TIME CMD
root        5887  3201  0 12:14 ?        00:00:00 nginx: master process /
usr/sbin/nginx
www-data    5918  5887  1 12:16 ?        00:00:01 nginx: worker process
www-data    5919  5887  3 12:16 ?        00:00:02 nginx: worker process
www-data    5920  5887  6 12:16 ?        00:00:03 nginx: worker process
www-data    5921  5887  3 12:16 ?        00:00:02 nginx: worker process
```

The new worker processes have picked up the new configuration now.

Reopening the log file

Reopening the log file is simple yet extremely important for the continuous operation of your server. When log file reopening is triggered with the USR1 signal, the master process of an instance takes the list of configured log files and opens each of them. If successful, it closes the old log files and signals worker processes to reopen the log files. Worker processes can now safely repeat the same procedure, and after that the log output is redirected to the new files. After that, worker processes close all old log file descriptors that they currently hold open.

> The paths to log files do not change during this procedure. Nginx expects that the old log files are renamed before triggering this function. That's why while opening log files with same paths, Nginx effectively creates or opens new files.

The steps of the log file reopening procedure are as follows:

1. Log files are renamed or moved to new locations via an external tool.
2. You send Nginx the USR1 signal. Nginx closes the old files and opens new ones.
3. Old files are now closed and can be archived.
4. New files are now active and being used.

A typical tool for managing Nginx log files is **logrotate**. The logrotate tool is a quite common tool that can be found in many Linux distributions. Here is an example configuration file for logrotate that automatically performs the log file rotation procedure:

```
/var/log/nginx/*.log {
        daily
        missingok
        rotate 7
        compress
        delaycompress
        notifempty
        create 640 nginx adm
        sharedscripts
        postrotate
                [ -f /var/run/nginx.pid ] && kill -USR1 `cat
/var/run/nginx.pid`
        endscript
}
```

The preceding script daily rotates each log file it can find in the `/var/log/nginx` folder. The log files are kept until seven files have accumulated. The `delaycompress` options specify that the log files should not be compressed immediately after rotation to avoid a situation where Nginx keeps writing to a file being compressed.

Problems in log file rotation procedure can lead to losses of data. Here is a checklist that will help you to configure your log file rotation procedure correctly:

- Make sure the `USR1` signal is delivered only after log files are moved. Failure to do so will make Nginx write to rotated files instead of new ones.

- Make sure Nginx has enough rights to create files in the log folder. If Nginx is not able to open new log files, the rotation procedure will fail.

Nginx binary upgrade

Nginx is capable of updating its own binary while operating. This is done by passing listening sockets to a new binary and listing to them in a special environment variable.

This function can be used to safely upgrade your binary on-the-fly to a new version or try out new features if you use a custom binary with plugins.

With other web servers, this operation would require stopping your server completely and starting it again with a new binary. Your service would be unavailable for a brief period. The Nginx binary upgrade function is used to avoid interruption of your service and provides a fall-back option if something goes wrong with the new binary.

To upgrade you binary, first make sure it has the same source code configuration as the old binary. Refer to the *Copying source code configuration from pre-built packages* section in *Chapter 1, Getting Started with Nginx,* to learn how to build a binary with source code configuration from another binary.

When the new binary is built, rename the old one and put the new binary into its place:

```
# mv /usr/sbin/nginx /usr/sbin/nginx.old
# mv objs/nginx /usr/sbin/nginx
```

The preceding sequence assumes your current working directory contains a Nginx source code tree.

Next, send the USR2 signal to the master process of the running instance:

```
# kill -USR2 12995
```

The master process will rename its PID file by adding an .oldbin suffix and start the new binary that will create a new master process. The new master process will read and parse the configuration and spawn new worker processes. The instance now looks like this:

```
UID         PID  PPID  C STIME TTY          TIME CMD
root       12995     1  0 13:28 ?        00:00:00 nginx: master process /
usr/sbin/nginx
www-data 12996 12995  0 13:28 ?        00:00:00 nginx: worker process
www-data 12997 12995  0 13:28 ?        00:00:00 nginx: worker process
www-data 12998 12995  0 13:28 ?        00:00:00 nginx: worker process
www-data 12999 12995  0 13:28 ?        00:00:00 nginx: worker process
root       13119 12995  0 13:30 ?        00:00:00 nginx: master process /
usr/sbin/nginx
www-data 13120 13119  2 13:30 ?        00:00:00 nginx: worker process
www-data 13121 13119  0 13:30 ?        00:00:00 nginx: worker process
www-data 13122 13119  0 13:30 ?        00:00:00 nginx: worker process
www-data 13123 13119  0 13:30 ?        00:00:00 nginx: worker process
```

In the preceding code, we can see two master processes: one for the old binary (12995) and one for the new binary (13119). The new master process inherits the listening sockets from the old master process, and workers of both instances accept incoming connections.

Graceful worker shutdown

In order to fully test-drive the new binary, we need to ask the old master process to gracefully shut down its worker processes. Once the new binary has started and the working processes of the new binary are running, send the master process of the old instance the WINCH signal using the following command:

```
# kill -WINCH 12995
```

Then, connections will be accepted only by workers of the new instance. The worker processes of the old instance will gracefully shut down:

```
UID          PID  PPID  C STIME TTY         TIME CMD
root       12995     1  0 13:28 ?        00:00:00 nginx: master process /
usr/sbin/nginx
www-data 12996 12995  2 13:28 ?        00:00:17 nginx: worker process is
shutting down
www-data 12998 12995  1 13:28 ?        00:00:13 nginx: worker process is
shutting down
www-data 12999 12995  2 13:28 ?        00:00:18 nginx: worker process is
shutting down
root       13119 12995  0 13:30 ?        00:00:00 nginx: master process /
usr/sbin/nginx
www-data 13120 13119  2 13:30 ?        00:00:18 nginx: worker process
www-data 13121 13119  2 13:30 ?        00:00:16 nginx: worker process
www-data 13122 13119  2 13:30 ?        00:00:12 nginx: worker process
www-data 13123 13119  2 13:30 ?        00:00:15 nginx: worker process
```

Finally, the worker processes of the old binary will quit and only the worker processes of the new binary will remain:

```
UID          PID  PPID  C STIME TTY         TIME CMD
root       12995     1  0 13:28 ?        00:00:00 nginx: master process /
usr/sbin/nginx
root       13119 12995  0 13:30 ?        00:00:00 nginx: master process /
usr/sbin/nginx
www-data 13120 13119  3 13:30 ?        00:00:20 nginx: worker process
www-data 13121 13119  3 13:30 ?        00:00:20 nginx: worker process
www-data 13122 13119  2 13:30 ?        00:00:16 nginx: worker process
www-data 13123 13119  2 13:30 ?        00:00:17 nginx: worker process
```

Now, only the worker processes of the new binary are accepting and processing incoming connections.

Finalizing the upgrade procedure

Once only the workers of the new binary are running, you have two choices.

If the new binary is working well, the old master process can be terminated by sending the QUIT signal:

```
# kill -QUIT 12995
```

The old master process will remove its PID file and the instance is now ready for the next upgrade. Later, if you find any issues with the new binary, you can downgrade to the old binary by repeating the whole binary upgrade procedure.

If the new binary is not working properly, you can restart the worker processes of the old master process by sending the HUP signal:

```
# kill -HUP 12995
```

The old master process will restart its working processes without re-reading the configuration files, and workers of both old and new binaries will now accept incoming connections:

```
# ps -C nginx -f
```

UID	PID	PPID	C	STIME	TTY	TIME	CMD
root usr/sbin/nginx	12995	1	0	13:28	?	00:00:00	nginx: master process /
root usr/sbin/nginx	13119	12995	0	13:30	?	00:00:00	nginx: master process /
www-data	13120	13119	4	13:30	?	00:01:25	nginx: worker process
www-data	13121	13119	4	13:30	?	00:01:29	nginx: worker process
www-data	13122	13119	4	13:30	?	00:01:21	nginx: worker process
www-data	13123	13119	4	13:30	?	00:01:27	nginx: worker process
www-data	13397	12995	4	14:02	?	00:00:00	nginx: worker process
www-data	13398	12995	0	14:02	?	00:00:00	nginx: worker process
www-data	13399	12995	0	14:02	?	00:00:00	nginx: worker process
www-data	13400	12995	0	14:02	?	00:00:00	nginx: worker process

The processes of the new binary can be gracefully shut down by sending the new master process the QUIT signal:

```
# kill -QUIT  13119
```

After that, you need to return the old binary back to its location:

```
# mv /usr/sbin/nginx.old /usr/sbin/nginx
```

The instance is now ready for the next upgrade.

 If a worker process is taking too long to quit for some reason, you can force it to quit by directly sending it the KILL signal.

If the new binary is not working properly and you need an urgent solution, you can urgently shut down the new master process by sending the TERM signal:

```
# kill -TERM  13119
```

The processes of the new binary will immediately quit. The old master process will be notified and it will start new worker processes. The old master process will also move its PID file back to its original location so that it replaces the PID file of the new binary. After that, you need to return the old binary back to its original location:

```
# mv /usr/sbin/nginx.old /usr/sbin/nginx
```

The instance is now ready for further operation or the next upgrade.

Handling difficult cases

In extremely rare cases, you might run into a difficult situation. If a worker process does not shut down when asked to in a reasonable time, there might be a problem with it. Typical signs of such problems are as follows:

- A process spends too much time in the running state (R) and does not shut down

- A process spends too much time in the noninterruptible sleep state (D) and does not shut down

- A process is sleeping (S) and does not shut down

In each of these cases, you can force the worker process to shut down by first sending the TERM signal directly to the worker process. If the worker process does not react within 30 seconds, you can force the process to quit by sending it the KILL signal.

Distribution-specific startup scripts

On Ubuntu, Debian, and RHEL, the startup script automates the preceding control sequences. By using the startup script, you don't need to remember the exact sequence of the commands and signal names. The following table illustrates the use of the startup script:

Command	Equivalent to
service nginx start	sbin/nginx
service nginx stop	TERM, wait 30 seconds, then KILL
service nginx restart	service nginx stop and service nginx start
service nginx configtest	nginx -t <config file>
service nginx reload	service nginx configtest and HUP
service nginx rotate	USR1
service nginx upgrade	USR2 and QUIT to the old master
service nginx status	show status of the instance

The binary upgrade procedure is limited to starting the new binary and signaling the old master process to gracefully shut down, so you don't have an option to test-drive the new binary in this case.

Allocating worker processes

We now consider recommendations on allocating worker processes. First, let's discuss a little bit about the background. Nginx is an asynchronous web server, which means actual input/output operations run asynchronously with the execution of a worker process. Each worker process runs an event loop that fetches all file descriptors that need processing using a special system call, and then services each of these file descriptors using nonblocking I/O operations. Hence, each worker process serves multiple connections.

In this situation, the time between an event occurs on a file descriptor, and this file descriptor can be serviced (that is latency) depends on how soon a full event processing cycle can be completed. Therefore, in order to achieve higher latency it makes sense to penalize the competition for CPU resources between worker processes in favor of more connections per process, because this would reduce the number of context switches between worker processes.

Therefore, *on the systems that are CPU-bound*, it makes sense to allocate as many worker processes as there are CPU cores in the system. For example, consider this output of the `top` command (this output can be obtained by pressing *1* on the keyboard after `top` starts):

```
top - 10:52:54 up 48 min,  2 users,  load average: 0.11, 0.18, 0.27
Tasks: 273 total,  2 running, 271 sleeping,  0 stopped,  0 zombie
%Cpu0  :  1.7 us,  0.3 sy,  0.0 ni, 97.7 id,  0.3 wa,  0.0 hi,  0.0 si,
0.0 st
%Cpu1  :  0.7 us,  0.3 sy,  0.0 ni, 94.7 id,  4.0 wa,  0.0 hi,  0.3 si,
0.0 st
%Cpu2  :  1.7 us,  1.0 sy,  0.0 ni, 97.3 id,  0.0 wa,  0.0 hi,  0.0 si,
0.0 st
%Cpu3  :  3.0 us,  1.0 sy,  0.0 ni, 95.0 id,  1.0 wa,  0.0 hi,  0.0 si,
0.0 st
%Cpu4  :  0.0 us,  0.0 sy,  0.0 ni,100.0 id,  0.0 wa,  0.0 hi,  0.0 si,
0.0 st
%Cpu5  :  0.3 us,  0.3 sy,  0.0 ni, 99.3 id,  0.0 wa,  0.0 hi,  0.0 si,
0.0 st
%Cpu6  :  0.3 us,  0.0 sy,  0.0 ni, 99.7 id,  0.0 wa,  0.0 hi,  0.0 si,
0.0 st
%Cpu7  :  0.0 us,  0.3 sy,  0.0 ni, 99.7 id,  0.0 wa,  0.0 hi,  0.0 si,
0.0 st
```

This system has eight independent CPU cores. The maximum number of worker processes that will not compete for CPU cores on this system is therefore eight. To configure Nginx to start a specified number of worker processes, you can use the `worker_processes` directive in the main configuration file:

```
worker_processes 8;
```

The preceding command will instruct Nginx to start eight worker processes to serve the incoming connections.

If the number of worker processes is set to a number lower than the number of CPU cores, Nginx will not be able to take advantage of all parallelism available in your system.

To extend the maximum number of connections that can be processed by a worker process, use the `worker_connections` directive:

```
events {
    worker_connections 10000;
}
```

The preceding command will extend the total number of connection that can be allocated to 10,000. This includes both inbound (connections from clients) and outbound connections (connections to proxied servers and other external resources).

On disk I/O-bound systems, in the absence of the AIO facility, additional latency might be introduced into the event cycle due to blocking disk I/O operations. While a worker process is waiting for a blocking disk I/O operation to complete on a certain file descriptor, the other file descriptors cannot be serviced. However, other processes can use the available CPU resources. Therefore, adding worker processes past the number of available I/O channels might not lead to an improvement in performance.

On systems with mixed resource demands, a worker process allocation strategy other than the previously mentioned two might be needed to achieve better performance. Try varying the numbers of workers in order to obtain the configuration that works best. This can range from one worker to hundreds of workers.

Setting up Nginx to serve static data

Now that you are more proficient in installing, configuring, and managing Nginx, we can proceed with some practical questions. Let's see how we can set up Nginx to serve static data such as images, CSS, or JavaScript files.

First, we will take the sample configuration from the previous chapter and make it support multiple virtual hosts using wild card inclusion:

```
error_log  logs/error.log;

worker_processes 8;

events {
    use epoll;
```

```
        worker_connections   10000;
    }


    http {
        include          mime.types;
        default_type     application/octet-stream;

        include /etc/nginx/site-enabled/*.conf;
    }
```

We have set up Nginx to take advantage of eight processor cores and include all configurations files located in /etc/nginx/site-enabled.

Next, we will configure a virtual host static.example.com for serving static data. The following content goes into the file /etc/nginx/site-enabled/static.example.com.conf:

```
    server {
        listen       80;
        server_name  static.example.com;

        access_log   /var/log/nginx/static.example.com-access.log   main;

        sendfile on;
        sendfile_max_chunk 1M;
        tcp_nopush on;
        gzip_static on;

        root /usr/local/www/static.example.com;
    }
```

This file configures virtual host static.example.com. The virtual host root location is set as /usr/local/www/static.example.com. To enable more efficient retrieval of static files, we encourage Nginx to use the sendfile() system call (sendfile on) and set the maximum sendfile chunk to 1 MB. We also enable the "TCP_NOPUSH" option to improve TCP segment utilization when using sendfile() (tcp_nopush on).

The gzip_static on directive instructs Nginx to check for gzipped copies of static files, such as main.js.gz for main.js and styles.css.gz for styles.css. If they are found, Nginx will indicate the presence of the .gzip content encoding, and use the content of the compressed files instead of the original one.

This configuration is suitable for virtual hosts that serve small-to-medium size static files.

Installing SSL certificates

Today, more than 60 percent of the HTTP traffic on the Internet is protected by SSL. In the presence of sophisticated attacks such as cache poisoning and DNS hijacking, SSL is mandatory if your web content has any value.

Nginx has high-class SSL support and makes it easy for you to configure. Let's walk over the installation procedure of an SSL virtual host.

Before we start, make sure the `openssl` package is installed on your system:

```
# apt-get install openssl
```

This will insure that you have the necessary tools to go over the SSL certificate issuing procedure.

Creating a Certificate Signing Request

You need an SSL certificate in order to set up an SSL virtual host. In order to obtain a real certificate, you need to contact a certification authority to issue an SSL certificate. A certification authority will usually charge you a fee for that.

To issue an SSL certificate, a certification authority needs a **Certificate Signing Request (CSR)** from you. A CSR is a message created by you and sent to a certification authority containing your identification data, such as distinguished name, address, and your public key.

To generate a CSR, run the following command:

```
openssl req -new -newkey rsa:2048 -nodes -keyout your_domain_name.key
-out your_domain_name.csr
```

This will start the process of generating two files: a private key for the decryption of your SSL certificate (`your_domain_name.key`) and a certificate signing request (`your_domain_name.csr`) used to apply for a new SSL certificate.

This command will ask you for your identification data:

- **Country name (C):** This is a two-letter country code, for example, NL or US.
- **State or province (S):** This is the full name of the state you or your company is in, for example, Noord-Holland.
- **Locality or city (L):** This is the city or town you or your company is in, for example, Amsterdam.

- **Organization (O)**: If your company or department has *&*, *@*, or any other symbol using the *Shift* key in its name, you must spell out the symbol or omit it to enroll. For example, XY & Z Corporation would be XYZ Corporation or XY and Z Corporation.

- **Organizational Unit (OU)**: This field is the name of the department or organization unit making the request.

- **Common name (CN)**: This is the full name of the host you are protecting.

The last field is of particular importance here. It must match the full name of the host you are protecting. For instance, if you registered a domain `example.com` and users will connect to `www.example.com`, you must enter `www.example.com` into the common name field. If you enter `example.com` into that field, the certificate will not be valid for `www.example.com`.

 Do not fill in optional attributes such as e-mail address, challenge password, or the optional company name when generating the CSR. They do not add much value, but just expose more personal data.

Your CSR is ready now. After you save your private key to some secure place, you can proceed with contacting a certification authority and enrolling for an SSL certificate. Present your CSR once requested.

Installing an issued SSL certificate

Once your certificate is issued, you can proceed with setting up your SSL server. Save your certificate under a descriptive name such as `your_domain_name.crt`. Move it to a secure directory that only Nginx and superuser have access to. We will use `/etc/ssl` for simplicity as an example of such a directory.

Now, you can start adding configuration for your secure virtual host:

```
server    {
        listen 443;
    server_name your.domain.com;
    ssl on;
    ssl_certificate /etc/ssl/your_domain_name.crt;
    ssl_certificate_key /etc/ssl/your_domain_name.key;
    [... the rest of the configuration ...]
}
```

The name of the domain in the `server_name` directive must match the value of the common name field in your certificate signing request.

After the configuration is saved, restart Nginx using the following command:

```
# service nginx restart
```

Navigate to `https://your.domain.com` to open a secure connection to your server now.

Permanently redirecting from a nonsecure virtual host

The preceding configuration handles only requests issued to the HTTPS service (port `443`) of your server. Most of the time, you will be running the plain HTTP service (port `80`) next to the secure one.

For a number of reasons, it's unwise to have different configurations for the plain HTTP and HTTPS services for the same host name. If certain resources are available over plain HTTP but not over SSL or the other way around, this might lead to bad references if a URL pointing to one of your resources is treated in a scheme-agnostic way.

Likewise, if certain resources are made available over both plain HTTP and SSL by mistake, then it is a security error because the resource can be obtained and interacted with in a nonsecure way by simply changing the `https://` scheme to `http://`.

To avoid these problems and to simplify your configuration, you can set up a simple permanent redirect from the non-SSL virtual host to the SSL virtual host:

```
server {
    listen      80;
    server_name  your.domain.com;

    rewrite ^/(.*)$ https://your.domain.com/$1 permanent;
}
```

This ensures that all requests over plain HTTP to any resource on your web site will be redirected to the identical resource on the SSL virtual host.

Managing temporary files

Managing temporary files is usually not a big deal, but you must be aware of it. Nginx uses temporary files to store transient data such as the following:

- Large request bodies received from users
- Large response bodies received from proxied servers or via FastCGI, SCGI, or UWCGI protocols.

In the *Installing Nginx* section of *Chapter 1, Getting Started with Nginx*, you saw the default location of temporary folders for these files. The following table lists the configuration directives that specify temporary folders for various Nginx core modules:

Directive	Purpose
`client_body_temp_path`	Specifies temporary path for client request body data
`proxy_temp_path`	Specifies temporary path for responses from proxied servers
`fastcgi_temp_path`	Specifies temporary path for responses from FastCGI servers
`scgi_temp_path`	Specifies temporary path for responses from SCGI servers
`uwsgi_temp_path`	Specifies temporary path for responses from UWCGI servers

The arguments of the preceding directives are as follows

```
proxy_temp_path <path> [<level1> [<level2> [<level3>]]]
```

In the preceding code, `<path>` specifies the path to the directory that contains temporary files, and the levels specify the number of characters in each level of hashed directories.

What is a hashed directory? In UNIX, a directory in the file system is essentially a file that simply contains a list of entries of that directory. So, imagine one of your temporary directories contains 100,000 entries. Each search in this directory routinely scans all of these 100,000 entries, which is not very efficient. To avoid this, you can split your temporary directory into a number of subdirectories, each of them containing a limited set of temporary files.

By specifying levels, you instruct Nginx to split your temporary directory into a set of subdirectories, each having a specified number of characters in its name, for example, a directive:

```
proxy_temp_path /var/lib/nginx/proxy 2;
```

The preceding line of code instructs Nginx to store a temporary file named 3924510929 under the path /var/lib/nginx/proxy/29/3924510929.

Likewise, the directive proxy_temp_path /var/lib/nginx/proxy 1 2 instructs Nginx to store a temporary file named 1673539942 under the path /var/lib/nginx/proxy/2/94/1673539942.

As you can see, the characters that constitute the names of the intermediary directories are extracted from the tail of the temporary file name.

Both hierarchical and nonhierarchical temporary directory structures have to be purged from time to time. This could be achieved by walking the directory tree and removing all files residing in those directories. You can use a command like the following one:

```
find /var/lib/nginx/proxy -type f -regex '.+/[0-9]+$' | xargs -I '{}' rm
"{}"
```

You can use the command from the interactive shell. This command will find all files ending with digits located in the temporary directory and remove each of these files by running rm. This command will prompt the removal if it finds something strange.

For the noninteractive mode, you can use a more dangerous command:

```
find /var/lib/nginx/proxy -type f -regex '.+/[0-9]+$' | xargs -I '{}' rm
-f "{}"
```

This command will not prompt the removal of files.

> This command is dangerous as it blindly removes a broadly-specified set of files. To avoid data loss, stick to the following principles when managing temporary directories:
> - Never store anything but temporary files inside temporary directories
> - Always use absolute paths in the first argument of a find command
> - If possible, check what you are about to remove by substituting rm with echo in order to print the list of files to be supplied to rm
> - Make sure Nginx stores temporary files under a specially-designated user such as nobody or www-data, and never under the superuser
> - Make sure the command above runs under a specially-designated user such as nobody or www-data, and never under the superuser

Communicating issues to developers

If you are running nonstable versions of Nginx for trial or using your own or third-party modules for Nginx, your instance might occasionally experience crashes. If you decide to communicate these issues to developers, here is a guide that will help you to do it most efficiently.

Developers usually don't have access to production systems, but knowing the environment your Nginx instance is running in is crucial to trace the cause of the problem.

Therefore, you need to provide detailed information about the issue. Detailed information about a crash can be found in the core file that was created after the crash.

Warning!

The core file contains a memory dump of a worker process at the moment of a crash and therefore can contain sensitive information, such as passwords, keys, or private data. Therefore, never share core files with people you don't trust.

Instead, use the following procedure to obtain detailed information about a crash:

1. Get a copy of the Nginx binary that you run with debugging information (see following instructions)

2. If a core file is available, run gdb on the binary with the debugging information:

   ```
   # gdb ./nginx-binary core
   ```

3. If the run is successful, this will open the gdb prompt. Type bt full in it:

   ```
   (gdb) bt full
   [… produces a dump … ]
   ```

The preceding command will produce a long dump of the stack at the moment of the crash and it's usually sufficient to debug a wide variety of problems. Make a summary of the configuration that resulted in a crash and send it over to the developer along with the full stack trace.

Creating a binary with debugging information

A detailed stack trace can be obtained only from a binary with debugging information. You don't necessarily need to run a binary with debugging information. It's only necessary to have a binary that is identical to the one that you run, but with extra debugging information on top of it.

It is possible to produce such a binary from the source code of the binary that you are running by configuring the source tree with an extra `-with-debug` option. The steps are as follows:

1. First, obtain configuration script arguments from the binary your instance is running:

    ```
    $ /usr/sbin/nginx -V
    ```

2. Add the `-with-debug` option in front of the argument string and run the configuration scripts:

    ```
    $ ./configure -with-debug --with-cc-opt='-g -O2 -fstack-protector
    --param=ssp-buffer-size=4 -Wformat -Werror=format-security -D_
    FORTIFY_SOURCE=2' --with-ld-opt='-Wl,-Bsymbolic-functions -Wl,-
    z,relro' …
    ```

Follow the remaining steps of the build procedure (refer to the previous chapter for details). Once you finish, a binary identical to the one that you are running but with debugging information appears in the `objs` directory of your source tree:

```
$ file objs/nginx

objs/nginx: ELF 32-bit LSB executable, Intel 80386, version 1 (SYSV),
dynamically linked (uses shared libs), for GNU/Linux 2.6.32, BuildID[sha1
]=7afba0f9be717c965a3cfaaefb6e2325bdcea676, not stripped
```

Now, you can use this binary to obtain a full stack trace from the core file produced by its twin binary.

Refer to the previous section in order to learn how to produce a stack trace.

Summary

In this chapter, you learned a lot of Nginx management techniques. We covered almost the full circle of Nginx operation, except for problem-dependent details. In the next and further chapters, you will start learning about particular features of Nginx and how to apply them. This will add some more flesh to your Nginx core skills.

3
Proxying and Caching

Designed as a web accelerator and a frontend server, Nginx has powerful tools
to delegate complex tasks to upstream servers while focusing on heavy lifting.
Reverse proxy is one such tool that turns Nginx into an essential component of
any high-performance web service.

By abstracting away complexities of HTTP and handling them in a scalable and
efficient manner, Nginx allows web applications to focus on solving the problem
they are designed to solve without stumbling upon low-level details.

In this chapter, you will learn:

- How to set up Nginx as a reverse proxy
- How to make proxying transparent for the upstream server and the end user
- How to handle upstream errors
- How to use Nginx cache

You will find out how to use all features of Nginx reverse proxy and turn it into a
powerful tool for accelerating and scaling your web service.

Nginx as a reverse proxy

HTTP is a complex protocol that deals with data of different modality and has
numerous optimizations that—if implemented properly—can lead to a significant
increase in web service performance.

At the same time, web application developers have less time to deal with low-level
issues and optimizations. The mere idea of decoupling a web application server
from a frontend server shifts the focus on managing incoming traffic to the frontend,
while shifting the focus on functionality, application logic, and features to the web
application server. This is where Nginx comes into play as a decoupling point.

An example of a decoupling point is SSL termination: Nginx receives and processes inbound SSL connections, it forwards the request over plain HTTP to an application server, and wraps the received response back into SSL. The application server no longer needs to take care of storing certificates, SSL sessions, handling encrypted and unencrypted transmission, and so on.

Other examples of decoupling are as follows:

- Efficient handling of static files and delegating the dynamic part to the upstream
- Rate, request, and connection limiting
- Compressing responses from the upstream
- Caching responses from the upstream
- Accelerating uploads and downloads

By shifting these functions to a Nginx-powered frontend, you are essentially investing in the reliability of your website.

Setting up Nginx as a reverse proxy

Nginx can be easily configured to work as a reverse proxy:

```
location /example {
    proxy_pass http://upstream_server_name;
}
```

In the preceding code, `upstream_server_name` is the host name of the upstream server. When a request for location is received, it will be passed to the upstream server with a specified host name.

If the upstream server does not have a host name, an IP address can be used instead:

```
location /example {
    proxy_pass http://192.168.0.1;
}
```

If the upstream server is listening on a nonstandard port, the port can be added to the destination URL:

```
location /example {
    proxy_pass http://192.168.0.1:8080;
}
```

The destination URL in the preceding examples does not have a path. This makes Nginx pass the request as is, without rewriting the path in the original request.

If a path is specified in the destination URL, it will replace a part of the path from the original request that corresponds to the matching part of the location. For example, consider the following configuration:

```
location /download {
    proxy_pass http://192.168.0.1/media;
}
```

If a request for /download/BigFile.zip is received, the path in the destination URL is /media and it corresponds to the matching /download part of the original request URI. This part will be replaced with /media before passing to the upstream server, so the passed request path will look like /media/BigFile.zip.

If proxy_pass directive is used inside a regex location, the matching part cannot be computed. In this case, a destination URI without a path must be used:

```
location ~* (script1|script2|script3)\.php$ {
    proxy_pass http://192.168.0.1;
}
```

The same applies to cases where the request path was changed with the rewrite directive and is used by a proxy_pass directive.

Variables can be a part of the destination URL as well:

```
location ~* ^/(index|content|sitemap)\.html$ {
    proxy_pass http://192.168.0.1/html/$1;
}
```

In fact, any part or even the whole destination URL can be specified by a variable:

```
location /example {
    proxy_pass $destination;
}
```

This gives enough flexibility in specifying the destination URL for the upstream server. In *Chapter 5, Managing Inbound and Outbound Traffic*, we will find out how to specify multiple servers as an upstream and distribute connections among them.

Setting the backend the right way

The right way to configure a backend is to avoid passing everything to it. Nginx has powerful configuration directives that help you ensure that only specific requests are delegated to the backend.

Consider the following configuration:

```
location ~* \.php$ {
    proxy_pass http://backend;
    [...]
}
```

This passes every request with a URI that ends with .php to the PHP interpreter. This is not only inefficient due to the intensive use of regular expressions, but also a serious security issue on most PHP setups because it may allow arbitrary code execution by an attacker.

Nginx has an elegant solution for this problem in the form of the try_files directive. The try_files directive takes a list of files and a location as the last argument. Nginx tries specified files in consecutive order and if none of them exists, it makes an internal redirect to the specified location. Consider the following example:

```
location / {
    try_files $uri $uri/ @proxy;
}

location @proxy {
    proxy_pass http://backend;
}
```

The preceding configuration first looks up a file corresponding to the request URI, looks for a directory corresponding to the request URI in the hope of returning an index of that directory, and finally makes an internal redirect to the named location @proxy if none of these files or directories exist.

This configuration makes sure that whenever a request URI points to an object in the filesystem it is handled by Nginx itself using efficient file operations, and only if there is no match in the filesystem for the given request URI is it delegated to the backend.

Adding transparency

Once forwarded to an upstream server, a request loses certain properties of the original request. For example, the virtual host in a forwarded request is replaced by the host/port combination of the destination URL. The forwarded request is received from an IP address of the Nginx proxy, and the upstream server's functionality based on the client's IP address might not function properly.

The forwarded request needs to be adjusted so that the upstream server can obtain the missing information of the original request. This can be easily done with the `proxy_set_header` directive:

```
proxy_set_header <header> <value>;
```

The `proxy_set_header` directive takes two arguments, the first of which is the name of the header that you want to set in the proxied request, and the second is the value for this header. Again, both arguments can contain variables.

Here is how you can pass the virtual host name from the original request:

```
location @proxy {
    proxy_pass http://192.168.0.1;
    proxy_set_header Host $host;
}
```

The variable `$host` has a smart functionality. It does not simply pass the virtual host name from the original request, but uses the name of the server the request is processed by if the host header of the original request is empty or missing. If you insist on using the bare virtual host name from the original request, you can use the `$http_host` variable instead of `$host`.

Now that you know how to manipulate the proxied request, we can let the upstream server know the IP address of the original client. This can be done by setting `X-Real-IP` and/or the `X-Forwarded-For` headers:

```
location @proxy {
    proxy_pass http://192.168.0.1;
    proxy_set_header Host $host;
    proxy_set_header X-Real-IP $remote_addr;
    proxy_set_header X-Forwarded-For $proxy_add_x_forwarded_for;
}
```

This will make the upstream server aware of the original client's IP address via `X-Real-IP` or the `X-Forwarded-For` header. Most application servers support this header and take appropriate actions to properly reflect the original IP address in their API.

Handling redirects

The next challenge is rewriting redirects. When the upstream server issues a temporary or permanent redirect (HTTP status codes `301` or `302`), the absolute URI in the location or refresh headers needs to be rewritten so that it contains a proper host name (the host name of the server the original request came to).

This can be done using the `proxy_redirect` directive:

```
location @proxy {
    proxy_pass http://localhost:8080;
    proxy_redirect http://localhost:8080/app http://www.example.com;
}
```

Consider a web application that is running at `http://localhost:8080/app`, while the original server has the address `http://www.example.com`. Assume the web application issues a temporary redirect (HTTP 302) to `http://localhost:8080/app/login`. With the preceding configuration, Nginx will rewrite the URI in the location header to `http://www.example.com/login`.

If the redirect URI was not rewritten, the client would be redirected to `http://localhost:8080/app/login`, which is valid only within a local domain, so the web application would not be able to work properly. With the `proxy_redirect` directive, the redirect URI will be properly rewritten by Nginx, and the web application will be able to perform the redirect properly.

The host name in the second argument of the `proxy_redirect` directive can be omitted:

```
location @proxy {
    proxy_pass http://localhost:8080;
    proxy_redirect http://localhost:8080/app /;
}
```

The preceding code can be further reduced to the following configuration using variables:

```
location @proxy {
    proxy_pass http://localhost:8080;
    proxy_redirect http://$proxy_host/app /;
}
```

The same transparency option can be applied to cookies. In the preceding example, consider cookies are set to the domain `localhost:8080`, since the application server replies at `http://localhost:8080`. The cookies will not be returned by the browser, because the cookie domain does not match the request domain.

Handling cookies

To make cookies work properly, the domain name in cookies needs to be rewritten by the Nginx proxy. To do this, you can use the `proxy_cookie_domain` directive as shown here:

```
location @proxy {
    proxy_pass http://localhost:8080;
    proxy_cookie_domain localhost:8080 www.example.com;
}
```

In the preceding example, Nginx replaces the cookie domain `localhost:8080` in the upstream response with `www.example.com`. The cookies set by the upstream server will refer to the domain `www.example.com` and the browser will return cookies in subsequent requests.

If cookie path needs to be rewritten as well due to application server being rooted at a different path, you can use the `proxy_cookie_path` directive as shown in the following code:

```
location @proxy {
    proxy_pass http://localhost:8080;
    proxy_cookie_path /my_webapp/ /;
}
```

In this example, whenever Nginx detects a cookie with a prefix specified in the first argument of the `proxy_cookie_path` directive (`/my_webapp/`), it replaces this prefix with the value in the second argument of the `proxy_cookie_path` directive (`/`).

Putting everything together for the `www.example.com` domain and the web application running at `localhost:8080`, we get the following configuration:

```
location @proxy {
    proxy_pass http://localhost:8080;
    proxy_set_header Host $host;
    proxy_set_header X-Real-IP $remote_addr;
    proxy_set_header X-Forwarded-For $proxy_add_x_forwarded_for;
    proxy_redirect http://$proxy_host/app /;
    proxy_cookie_domain $proxy_host www.example.com;
    proxy_cookie_path /my_webapp/ /;
}
```

The preceding configuration ensures transparency for a web application server so that it doesn't even need to know which virtual host it is running on.

Using SSL

If the upstream server supports SSL, connections to the upstream server can be secured by simply changing the destination URL scheme to `https`:

```
location @proxy {
    proxy_pass https://192.168.0.1;
}
```

If the authenticity of the upstream server needs to be verified, this can be enabled using the `proxy_ssl_verify` directive:

```
location @proxy {
    proxy_pass https://192.168.0.1;
    proxy_ssl_verify on;
}
```

The certificate of the upstream server will be verified against certificates of well-known certification authorities. In Unix-like operating systems, they are usually stored in `/etc/ssl/certs`.

If an upstream uses a trusted certificate that cannot be verified by well-known certification authorities or a self-signed certificate, it can be specified and declared as trusted using the `proxy_ssl_trusted_certificate` directive. This directive specifies the path to the certificate of the upstream server or a certificate chain required to authenticate the upstream server in PEM format. Consider the following example:

```
location @proxy {
    proxy_pass https://192.168.0.1;
    proxy_ssl_verify on;
    proxy_ssl_trusted_certificate /etc/nginx/upstream.pem;
}
```

If Nginx needs to authenticate itself to the upstream server, the client certificate and the key can be specified using the `proxy_ssl_certificate` and `proxy_ssl_certificate_key` directives. The directive `proxy_ssl_certificate` specifies the path to the client certificate in PEM format, while `proxy_ssl_certificate_key` specifies the path to the private key from the client certificate in PEM format. Consider the following example:

```
location @proxy {
    proxy_pass https://192.168.0.1;
    proxy_ssl_certificate /etc/nginx/client.pem;
    proxy_ssl_certificate_key /etc/nginx/client.key;
}
```

The specified certificate will be presented while setting up the secure connection to the upstream server, and its authenticity will be verified by specified private key.

Handling errors

If Nginx experiences a problem contacting the upstream server or the upstream server returns an error, there is an option to take certain actions.

The upstream server connectivity errors can be handled using the `error_page` directive:

```
location ~* (script1|script2|script3)\.php$ {
    proxy_pass http://192.168.0.1;
    error_page 500 502 503 504 /50x.html;
}
```

This will make Nginx return the document from the file `50x.html` once an upstream connectivity error has occurred.

This will not change the HTTP status code in the response. To change the HTTP status code to successful, you can use the following syntax:

```
location ~* (script1|script2|script3)\.php$ {
    proxy_pass http://192.168.0.1;
    error_page 500 502 503 504 =200 /50x.html;
}
```

A more sophisticated action can be taken upon failure of an upstream server using an `error_page` directive that points to a named location:

```
location ~* (script1|script2|script3)\.php$ {
    proxy_pass http://upstreamA;
    error_page 500 502 503 504 @retry;
}

location @retry {
    proxy_pass http://upstreamB;
    error_page 500 502 503 504 =200 /50x.html;
}
```

In the preceding configuration, Nginx first tries to fulfill the request by forwarding it to the `upstreamA` server. If this results in an error, Nginx switches to a named location `@retry` in an attempt to try with the `upstreamB` server. Request an URI while switching so that the `upstreamB` server will receive an identical request. If this doesn't help either, Nginx returns a static file `50x.html` pretending no error occurred.

If an upstream has replied but returned an error, it can be intercepted rather than passed to the client using the `proxy_intercept_errors` directive:

```
location ~* (script1|script2|script3)\.php$ {
    proxy_pass http://upstreamA;
    proxy_intercept_errors on;
    error_page 500 502 503 504 403 404 @retry;
}

location @retry {
    proxy_pass http://upstreamB;
    error_page 500 502 503 504 =200 /50x.html;
}
```

In the preceding configuration, the `upstreamB` server will be called even when the `upstreamA` server replies but returns erroneous HTTP status code, such as `403` or `404`. This gives `upstreamB` an opportunity to fix the soft errors of `upstreamA`, if necessary.

However, this configuration pattern must not proliferate too much. In *Chapter 5, Managing Inbound and Outbound Traffic*, we will find out how to handle such situations in a more elegant way, without sophisticated configuration structures.

Choosing an outbound IP address

Sometimes, when your proxy server has multiple network interfaces, it becomes necessary to choose which IP address should be used as outbound address for upstream connections. By default, the system will choose the address of the interface that adjoins the network containing the host used as destination in the default route.

To choose a particular IP address for outbound connections, you can use the `proxy_bind` directive:

```
location @proxy {
    proxy_pass https://192.168.0.1;
    proxy_bind 192.168.0.2;
}
```

This will make Nginx bind outbound sockets to the IP address `192.168.0.2` before making a connection. The upstream server will then see connections coming from IP address `192.168.0.2`.

Accelerating downloads

Nginx is very efficient at heavy operations, such as handling large uploads and downloads. These operations can be delegated to Nginx using built-in functionality and third-party modules.

To accelerate download, the upstream server must be able to issue the `X-Accel-Redirect` header that points to the location of a resource which needs to be returned, instead of the response obtained from the upstream. Consider the following configuration:

```
location ~* (script1|script2|script3)\.php$ {
    proxy_pass https://192.168.0.1;
}

location /internal-media/ {
    internal;
    alias /var/www/media/;
}
```

With the preceding configuration, once Nginx detects the `X-Accel-Redirect` header in the upstream response, it performs an internal redirect to the location specified in this header. Assume the upstream server instructs Nginx to perform an internal redirect to `/internal-media/BigFile.zip`. This path will be matched against the location `/internal-media`. This location specifies the document root at `/var/www/media`. So if a file `/var/www/media/BigFile.zip` exists, it will be returned to the client using efficient file operations.

For many web application servers, this feature provides an enormous speed up—both because they might not handle large downloads efficiently and because proxying reduces efficiency of large downloads.

Caching

Once Nginx is set up as a reverse proxy, it's logical to turn it into a caching proxy. Fortunately, this can be achieved very easily with Nginx.

Configuring caches

Before you can enable caching for a certain location, you need to configure a cache. A cache is a filesystem directory containing files with cached items and a shared memory segment where information about cached items is stored.

A cache can be declared using the `proxy_cache_path` directive:

```
proxy_cache_path <path> keys_zone=<name>:<size> [other
parameters...];
```

The preceding command declares a cache rooted at the path `<path>` with a shared memory segment named `<name>` of the size `<size>`.

This directive has to be specified in the `http` section of the configuration. Each instance of the directive declares a new cache and must specify a unique name for a shared memory segment. Consider the following example:

```
http {
    proxy_cache_path /var/www/cache keys_zone=my_cache:8m;
    [...]
}
```

The preceding configuration declares a cache rooted at `/var/www/cache` with a shared memory segment named `my_cache`, which is 8 MB in size. Each cache item takes around 128 bytes in memory, thus the preceding configuration allocates space for around 64,000 items.

The following table lists other parameters of `proxy_cache_path` and their meaning:

Parameter	Description
`levels`	Specifies hierarchy levels of the cache directory
`inactive`	Specifies the time after which a cache item will be removed from the cache if it was not used, regardless of freshness
`max_size`	Specifies maximum size (total size) of all cache items
`loader_files`	Specifies the number of files a **cache loader** process loads in each iteration
`loader_sleep`	Specifies the time interval a cache loader process sleeps between each iteration
`loader_threshold`	Specifies the time limit for each iteration of a cache loader process

Once Nginx starts, it processes all configured caches and allocates shared memory segments for each of the caches.

After that, a special process called cache loader takes care of loading cached items into memory. Cache loader loads items in iterations. The parameters `loader_files`, `loader_sleep`, and `loader_threshold` define the behavior of the cache loader process.

When running, a special process called **cache manager** monitors the total disk space taken by all cache items and evicts less requested items if the total consumed space is larger than specified in the max_size parameter.

Enabling caching

To enable caching for a location, you need to specify the cache using the proxy_cache directive:

```
location @proxy {
    proxy_pass http://192.168.0.1:8080;
    proxy_cache my_cache;
}
```

The argument of the proxy_cache directive is the name of a shared memory segment that points to one of the caches configured using the proxy_cache_path directive. The same cache can be used in multiple locations. The upstream response will be cached if it is possible to determine the expiration interval for it. The primary source for the expiration interval for Nginx is the upstream itself. The following table explains which upstream response header influences caching and how:

Upstream response header	How it influences caching
X-Accel-Expires	This specifies the cache item expiration interval in seconds. If the value starts from @, then the number following it is UNIX timestamp when the item is due to expire. This header has the higher priority.
Expires	This specifies the cache item expiration time stamp.
Cache-Control	This enables or disables caching
Set-Cookie	This disables caching
Vary	The special value * disables caching.

It is also possible to explicitly specify an expiration interval for various response codes using the proxy_cache_valid directive:

```
location @proxy {
    proxy_pass http://192.168.0.1:8080;
    proxy_cache my_cache;
    proxy_cache_valid 200 301 302 1h;
}
```

This sets the expiration interval for responses with codes 200, 301, 302 to 1h (1 hour). Note that the default status code list for the `proxy_cache_valid` directive is 200, 301, and 302, so the preceding configuration can be simplified as follows:

```
location @proxy {
    proxy_pass http://192.168.0.1:8080;
    proxy_cache my_cache;
    proxy_cache_valid 10m;
}
```

To enable caching for negative responses, such as 404, you can extend the status code list in the `proxy_cache_valid` directive:

```
location @proxy {
    proxy_pass http://192.168.0.1:8080;
    proxy_cache my_cache;
    proxy_cache_valid 200 301 302 1h;
    proxy_cache_valid 404 1m;
}
```

The preceding configuration will cache 404 responses for 1m (1 minute). The expiration interval for negative responses is deliberately set to much lower values than that of the positive responses. Such an optimistic approach ensures higher availability by expecting negative responses to improve, considering them as transient and assuming a shorter expected lifetime.

Choosing a cache key

Choosing the right cache key is important for the best operation of the cache. The cache key must be selected such that it maximizes the expected efficiency of the cache, provided that each cached item has valid content for all subsequent requests that evaluate to the same key. This requires some explanation.

First, let's consider efficiency. When Nginx refers to the upstream server in order to revalidate a cache item, it obviously stresses the upstream server. With each subsequent cache hit, Nginx reduces the stress on the upstream server in comparison to the situation when requests were forwarded to the upstream without caching. Thus, the efficiency of the cache can be represented as *Efficiency = (Number hits + Number misses) / Number misses.*

Thus, when nothing can be cached, each request leads to a cache miss and the efficiency is 1. But when we get 99 subsequent cache hits for each cache miss, the efficiency evaluates to *(99 + 1) / 1 = 100*, which is 100 times larger!

Second, if a document is cached but it is not valid for all requests that evaluate to the same key, clients might see content that is not valid for their requests.

For example, the upstream analyses the `Accept-Language` header and returns the version of the document in the most suitable language. If the cache key does not include the language, the first user to request the document will obtain it in their language and trigger the caching in that language. All users that subsequently request this document will see the cached version of the document, and thus they might see it in the wrong language.

If the cache key includes the language of the document, the cache will contain multiple separate items for the same document in each requested language, and all users will see it in the proper language.

The default cache key is `$scheme$proxy_host$request_uri`.

This might not be optimal because of the following reasons:

- The web application server at `$proxy_host` can be responsible for multiple domains
- The HTTP and HTTPS versions of the website can be identical (`$scheme` variable is redundant, thus duplicating items in the cache)
- Content can vary depending on query arguments

Thus, considering everything described previously and given that HTTP and HTTPS versions of the website are identical and content varies depending on query arguments, we can set the cache key to a more optimal value `$host$request_uri$is_args$args`. To change the default cache item key, you can use the `proxy_cache_key` directive:

```
location @proxy {
    proxy_pass http://192.168.0.1:8080;
    proxy_cache my_cache;
    proxy_cache_key "$host$uri$is_args$args";
}
```

This directive takes a script as its argument which is evaluated into a value of a cache key at runtime.

Improving cache efficiency and availability

The efficiency and availability of the cache can be improved. You can prevent an item from being cached until it gets a certain minimum number of requests. This could be achieved using the `proxy_cache_min_uses` directive:

```
location @proxy {
    proxy_pass http://192.168.0.1:8080;
    proxy_cache my_cache;
    proxy_cache_min_uses 5;
}
```

In the preceding example, the response will be cached once the item gets no less than five requests. This prevents the cache from being populated by infrequently used items, thus reducing the disk space used for caching.

Once the item has expired, it can be revalidated without being evicted. To enable revalidation, use the `proxy_cache_revalidate` directive:

```
location @proxy {
    proxy_pass http://192.168.0.1:8080;
    proxy_cache my_cache;
    proxy_cache_revalidate on;
}
```

In the preceding example, once a cache item expires, Nginx will revalidate it by making a conditional request to the upstream server. This request will include the `If-Modified-Since` and/or `If-None-Match` headers as a reference to the cached version. If the upstream server responds with a `304 Not Modified` response, the cache item remains in the cache and the expiration time stamp is reset.

Multiple simultaneous requests can be prohibited from filling the cache at the same time. Depending on the upstream reaction time, this might speed up cache population while reducing the load on the upstream server at the same time. To enable this behavior, you can use the `proxy_cache_lock` directive:

```
location @proxy {
    proxy_pass http://backend;
    proxy_cache my_cache;
    proxy_cache_lock on;
}
```

Once the behavior is enabled, only one request will be allowed to populate a cache item it is related to. The other requests related to this cache item will wait until either the cache item is populated or the lock timeout expires. The lock timeout can be specified using the `proxy_cache_lock_directive` directive.

If higher availability of the cache is required, you can configure Nginx to reply with stale data when a request refers to a cached item. This is very useful when Nginx acts as an edge server in a distribution network. The users and search engine crawlers will see your web site available, even though the main site experiences connectivity problems. To enable replying with stale data, use the `proxy_cache_use_stale` directive:

```
location @proxy {
    proxy_pass http://backend;
    proxy_cache my_cache;
    proxy_cache_use_stale error timeout http_500 http_502 http_503
http_504;
}
```

The preceding configuration enables replying with stale data in case of connectivity error, upstream error (502, 503, or 504), and connection timeout. The following table lists all possible values for arguments of the `proxy_cache_use_stale` directive:

Value	Meaning
error	A connection error has occurred or an error during sending a request or receiving a reply has occurred
timeout	A connection timed out during setup, sending a request or receiving a reply
invalid_header	The upstream server has returned an empty or invalid reply
updating	Enables stale replies while the cache item is being updated
http_500	The upstream server returned a reply with HTTP status code 500 (Internal Server Error)
http_502	The upstream server returned a reply with HTTP status code 502 (Bad Gateway)
http_503	The upstream server returned a reply with HTTP status code 503 (Service Unavailable)
http_504	The upstream server returned a reply with HTTP status code 504 (Gateway Timeout)
http_403	The upstream server returned a reply with HTTP status code 403 (Forbidden)
http_404	The upstream server returned a reply with HTTP status code 404 (Not Found)
off	Disables use of stale replies

Handling exceptions and borderline cases

When caching is not desirable or not efficient, it can be bypassed or disabled. This can happen in the following instances:

- A resource is dynamic and varies depending on external factors

- A resource is user-specific and varies depending on cookies

- Caching does not add much value

- A resource is not static, for example a video stream

When bypass is forced, Nginx forwards the request to the backend without looking up an item in the cache. The bypass can be configured using the `proxy_cache_bypass` directive:

```
location @proxy {
    proxy_pass http://backend;
    proxy_cache my_cache;
    proxy_cache_bypass $do_not_cache $arg_nocache;
}
```

This directive can take one or more arguments. When any of them evaluate to true (nonempty value and not 0), Nginx does not look up an item in the cache for a given request. Instead, it directly forwards the request to the upstream server. The item can still be stored in the cache.

To prevent an item from being stored in the cache, you can use the `proxy_no_cache` directive:

```
location @proxy {
    proxy_pass http://backend;
    proxy_cache my_cache;
    proxy_no_cache $do_not_cache $arg_nocache;
}
```

This directive works exactly like the `proxy_cache_bypass` directive, but prevents items from being stored in the cache. When only the `proxy_no_cache` directive is specified, the items can still be returned from the cache. The combination of both `proxy_cache_bypass` and `proxy_no_cache` disables caching completely.

Now, let's consider a real-world example when caching needs to be disabled for all user-specific pages. Assume that you have a website powered by WordPress and you want to enable caching for all pages but disable caching for all customized or user-specific pages. To implement this, you can use a configuration similar to the following:

```
location ~* wp\-.*\.php|wp\-admin {
    proxy_pass http://backend;

    proxy_set_header Host $http_host;
    proxy_set_header X-Real-IP $remote_addr;
}

location / {
    if ($http_cookie ~* "comment_author_|wordpress_|wp-postpass_" ) {
        set $do_not_cache 1;
    }

    proxy_pass http://backend;

    proxy_set_header Host $http_host;
    proxy_set_header X-Real-IP $remote_addr;

    proxy_cache my_cache;
    proxy_cache_bypass $do_not_cache;
    proxy_no_cache $do_not_cache;
}
```

In the preceding configuration, we first delegate all requests pertaining to the WordPress administrative area to the upstream server. We then use the `if` directive to look up WordPress login cookies and set the `$do_not_cache` variable to 1 if they are present. Then, we enable caching for all other locations but disable caching whenever the `$do_not_cache` variable is set to 1 using the `proxy_cache_bypass` and `proxy_no_cache` directives. This disables caching for all requests with WordPress login cookies.

The preceding configuration can be extended to extract no-cache flags from arguments or HTTP headers, to further tune your caching.

Summary

In this chapter, you learned how to work with proxying and caching—some of the most important Nginx features. These features practically define Nginx as a web accelerator and being proficient in them is essential to get the most out of Nginx.

In the next chapter, we'll look into how to rewrite engine works in Nginx and the basics of access control.

4

Rewrite Engine and Access Control

The World Wide Web and HTTP as its building block operate in URLs. Since URLs are so fundamental, the ability of a server to manipulate URLs is essential.

Nginx allows you to manipulate URLs using a built-in rewrite engine. The Nginx rewrite engine has a broad functionality and is very easy to configure, which makes it a very powerful tool. We'll walk through the entire rewrite engine in this chapter.

Another topic that we are going to explore in this chapter is access control. This is, obviously, an essential function of every software system that keeps the system secure and reliable. We'll walk through access control methods available in Nginx and explore their subtleties, and you'll learn how to combine them.

The basics of the rewrite engine

The rewrite engine allows you to manipulate the request URI of inbound requests.

The rewrite engine is configured using rewrite rules. Rewrite rules are used when the request URI needs to undergo transformation before further processing. Rewrite rules instruct Nginx to match the request URI with a regular expression and substitute the request URI with a specified pattern whenever a match has been scored.

Rewrite rules can be specified inside `server`, `location`, and `if` sections of the configuration.

Let's study some examples of rewrite rules in action. Consider a simple case when one resource needs to be substituted by another:

```
location / {
    rewrite ^/css/default\.css$ /css/styles.css break;
    root /var/www/example.com;
}
```

With the preceding configuration, every request to /css/default.css will have its URI rewritten to /css/styles.css and will fetch this resource instead. The rewrite directive specifies a pattern that has to match the request URI in order to fire the rule and a substitution string that says how the request URI must look after transformation. The third argument, break, is a flag that instructs Nginx to stop processing rewrite rules once a match for this rule has been scored.

The preceding configuration can be extended to work with multiple resources as well. For that, you need to use captures (round brackets in the first argument) and positional parameters (variables with numbers that refer to captures):

```
location / {
    rewrite ^/styles/(.+)\.css$ /css/$1.css break;
    root /var/www/example.com;
}
```

With the preceding configuration, every request to any CSS file in /styles/ will have its URI rewritten to the corresponding resource in /css/.

In the last two examples, we used the break flag in order to stop rewrite rules from processing as soon as a match is found (assuming more rules can be added to those configurations). If we want to combine those two examples, we need to drop the break flag and allow the cascading application of rewrite rules:

```
location / {
    rewrite ^/styles/(.+)\.css$ /css/$1.css;
    rewrite ^/css/default\.css$ /css/styles.css;
    root /var/www/example.com;
}
```

Now, every request to style sheets in /styles/ will be redirected to the corresponding resource in /css/, and /css/default.css will be rewritten to /css/styles.css. A request to /styles/default.css will undergo two rewrites, as it sequentially matches both rules.

Notice that all URI transformations are performed by Nginx internally. This means that for an external client, the original URIs return ordinary resources, thus the previous configurations will externally look like a series of documents with identical content (that is, `/css/default.css` will be identical to `/css/styles.css`).

This is not a desirable effect in the case of ordinary web pages, as search engines might penalize your website for duplicate content.

To avoid this problem, it is necessary to replace copies of a resource with permanent redirects to the master resource, as shown in the following configuration:

```
location / {
    rewrite ^/styles/(.+)\.css$ /css/$1.css permanent;
    root /var/www/example.com;
}
```

This works well for whole sections of a website:

```
location / {
    rewrite ^/download/(.+)$ /media/$1 permanent;
    root /var/www/example.com;
}
```

It also works for an entire virtual host:

```
server {
    listen 80;
    server_name example.com;
    rewrite ^/(.*)$ http://www.example.com/$1 permanent;
}
```

The preceding configuration for any URL requested performs a permanent redirect from a top-level domain `example.com` to the www sub domain, making it the primary entry point of the website.

The next powerful application of rewrite rules is translating a semantic URL into a URL with a query (section of a URL after the ? character). This functionality has its primary application in **Search Engine Optimization (SEO)** and website usability, and it is driven by a need to obtain semantic URLs for each and every resource and to deduplicate the content.

 You can find more information about semantic URLs at https://en.wikipedia.org/wiki/Semantic_URL.

Consider the following configuration:

```
server {
    [...]
    rewrite ^/products/$ /products.php last;
    rewrite ^/products/(.+)$ /products.php?name=$1 last;
    rewrite
  ^/products/(.+)/(.+)/$ /products.php?name=$1&page=$2 last;
    [...]
}
```

The preceding configuration transforms URLs consisting of a number of path sections starting with /products into a URL starting with /products.php and arguments. In this way, it is possible to hide implementation details from users and search engines, and generate semantic URLs.

Note that the flags of the rewrite directives are now set to last. This makes Nginx seek a new location for a rewritten URL and process request with a newly-found location.

Now that you have studied some examples of rewrite rules in action, you can learn more about the nitty-gritty details in order to master the rewrite rule. The following sections take a deeper look at its syntax and functionality.

More about rewrite rules

Now, let's discuss some of interesting details of the rewrite rules. Here's the complete syntax of the rewrite directive:

```
rewrite <pattern> <substitution> [<flag>];
```

The first argument of this directive, <pattern>, is a regular expression that needs to match the request URI in order to activate the substitution. The <substitution> argument is a script that is evaluated once a match has been scored and the value produced by evaluation replaces the request URI. Special variables $1...$9 can be used to cross-reference a pattern and its substitution by referring to a capture with the specified position. The <flag> argument affects the behavior of the rewrite directive. The following table lists all possible flags of the rewrite directive and their functions:

Flag	Function
break	Interrupts processing of rewrite rules
last	Interrupts processing of rewrite rules and looks up a location for the new request URI

Flag	Function
redirect	Returns a temporary redirect (HTTP status 302) to the new request URI
permanent	Returns a permanent redirect (HTTP status 301) to the new request URI

The rewrite engine makes multiple passes before a location for the request is found, and then in the request location and subsequent locations that the request is redirected to (such as those that are invoked by the error_page directive).

Rewrite rules specified directly in the server section are processed in the first pass, while rewrite rules in the location, if, and other sections within the server section are processed at subsequent passes. Consider the following example:

```
server {
    <rewrite rules here are processed in the first pass>;

    location /a {
        <rewrite rules here are processed in subsequent passes>;
    }
    location /b {
        <rewrite rules here are processed in subsequent passes>;
    }
}
```

After the first pass is complete, Nginx searches for a location that matches the rewritten request URI if a rewrite was performed, or a location that matches the original request URI (if no rewrite took place). The subsequent passes alter the request URI without changing the location.

Rewrite rules at each pass are processed in order of appearance. Once a match is scored, the substitution is applied and processing resumes with subsequent rewrite rules—unless a flag is specified to interrupt processing.

If the resulting request URI starts with http:// or https://, it is treated as absolute and Nginx returns a temporary (302 "Found") or a permanent (301 "Moved Permanently") redirect to the resulting location.

Patterns

Now, let's go back to the `<pattern>` argument and see how a match pattern can be specified. The following table gives a brief overview of regular expression syntax used in rewrite rules:

Pattern	Examples	Description
`<pattern A>` `<pattern B>`	`Ab, (aa)(bb)`	Following
`<pattern A> |` `<pattern B>`	`a|b, (aa)|(bb)`	Alternative
`<pattern>?`	`(\.gz)?`	Option
`<pattern>*`	`A*, (aa)*`	Repetition of `<pattern>` from *0* to *infinity*
`<pattern>+`	`a+, (aa)+`	Repetition of `<pattern>` from *1* to *infinity*
`<pattern>{n}`	`a{5}, (aa){6}`	Repetition of `<pattern>` *n* times
`<pattern>{n,}`	`a{3,}, (aa){7,}`	Repetition of `<pattern>` from *n* to *infinity*
`<pattern>{,m}`	`a{,6}, (aa){,3}`	Repetition of `<pattern>` from *0* to *m*
`<pattern>{n,m}`	`a{5,6}, (aa){1,3}`	Repetition of `<pattern>` from *n* to *m*
`( <pattern> )`	`(aa)`	Grouping or parameter capture
`.`	`.+`	Any character
`^`	`^/index`	Start of line
`$`	`\.php$`	End of line
`[<characters>]`	`[A-Za-z]`	Any character from the specified set
`[^<characters>]`	`[^0-9]`	Any character outside of the specified set

The patterns are listed in increasing priority order. That is, the pattern `aa|bb` will be interpreted as `a(a|b)b`, while the pattern `a{5}aa{6}` will be interpreted as `(a{5}) (a) (a{6})` and so on.

To specify characters that are themselves part of regular expression syntax, you can use the backslash character `\`, for example `\*` will match an asterisk `*`, `\.` will match a dot character `.`, `\\` will match the backslash character itself and `\{` will match an opening curly bracket `{`.

More information about regular expression syntax in rewrite rules can be found on the PCRE website `www.pcre.org`.

Captures and positional parameters

Captures are designated with round brackets and mark sections of matched URLs that need to be extracted. Positional parameters refer to substrings of the matched URLs extracted by corresponding capture, that is, if the pattern is as follows:

```
^/users/(.+)/(.+)/$
```

Also, if the request URL is like this:

```
/users/id/23850/
```

The positional parameters `$1` and `$2` will evaluate to `id` and `23850`, respectively. Positional parameters can be used in any order within the substitution string and this is how you connect it with the match pattern.

Other functionalities of the rewrite engine

The rewrite engine can also be used to perform other tasks:

- Assigning variables
- Evaluating predicates using the `if` directive
- Replying with specified HTTP status code

A combination of these operations and rewrite rules can be performed at every pass of the rewrite engine. Note that `if` sections are separate locations, so it is still possible that the location will change at the location rewrite pass.

Assigning variables

Variables can be assigned using the `set` directive:

```
set $fruit "apple";
```

Variable values can be scripts with text and other variables:

```
set $path "static/$arg_filename";
```

Once set on the rewrite phase, variables can be used in any directive in the rest of the configuration file.

Evaluating predicates using if sections

You have probably figured out from the title that `if` sections are part of the rewrite engine. This is true. The `if` sections can be used to conditionally apply selected rewrite rules:

```
if ( $request_method = POST ) {
    rewrite ^/media/$ /upload last;
}
```

In the preceding configuration, any attempt to make a POST request to the URL /media/ will result in rewriting it to the URL /upload, while requests with other methods to the same URL will result in no rewrites. Multiple conditions can also be combined. Let's look at the following code:

```
set $c1 "";
set $c2 "";

if ( $request_method = POST ) {
    set $c1 "yes";
}

if ( $scheme = "https" ) {
    set $c2 "yes";
}

set $and "${c1}_${c2}";

if ( $and = "yes_yes" ) {
    rewrite [...];
}
```

The preceding configuration applies the rewrite only when both `if` conditions are fulfilled, that is, when the request method is POST and the request URL scheme is https.

Now that you know how you can use the `if` section, let's talk about its side effects. Remember that conditions in the `if` directives are evaluated in the course of the `rewrite` directive processing. What it means is that when the `if` section contains directives that are not part of the rewrite engine, the behavior of the `if` section becomes non-intuitive. This was discussed in *Chapter 1, Getting Started with Nginx*. Consider the following configuration:

```
if ( $request_method = POST ) {
    set $c1 "yes";
    proxy_pass http://localhost:8080;
```

```
    }

if ( $scheme = "https" ) {
    set $c2 "yes";
    gzip on
}
```

Each individual `if` section contains an atomic set of configuration settings.
Assume Nginx receives a POST request with the `https` URL scheme such that both
conditions evaluate to true. All `set` directives will be correctly processed by the
rewrite engine and will be assigned to proper values. However, Nginx cannot merge
other configuration settings and cannot have multiple configurations active at once.
When rewrite processing is finished, Nginx simply switches configuration to the last
`if` section with its conditions evaluated to true. Because of that, in the preceding
configuration, compression will be switched on but the request will not be proxied
according to `proxy_pass` directive. This is not something you might expect.

To avoid this non-intuitive behavior, stick to the following best practices:

- Minimize the usage of the `if` directive
- Combine the `if` evaluations using the `set` directive
- Take actions only in the last `if` section.

Replying with a specified HTTP status code

If a definite reply with a specified HTTP status code is required in a certain location,
you can use the `return` directive to enable this behavior and specify the status
code, a reply body, or a redirect URL. Let's look at the following code:

```
location / {
    return 301 "https://www.example.com$uri";
}
```

The preceding configuration will execute a permanent redirect (301) to the secure
part of domain `www.example.com` and the URI path identical to the URI path in the
original request. Thus, the second argument of the `return` directive will be treated as
a redirect URI. The other status codes that treat the second argument of the `return`
directive as a redirect URI are `302`, `303` and `307`.

> Performing a redirect with the `return` directive is much faster than
> doing so with the `rewrite` directive, because it does not run any
> regular expressions. Use the `return` directive in your configuration
> instead of the `rewrite` directive whenever possible.

The status code 302 is quite common, so the `return` directive has a simplified syntax for temporary redirects:

```
location / {
    return "https://www.example.com$uri";
}
```

As you can see, if the `return` directive has a single argument, it is treated as redirect URI and makes Nginx perform a temporary redirect. This argument must start from `http://` or `https://` to trigger such behavior.

The `return` directive can be used to return a reply with a specified body. To trigger such behavior, the status code must simply be other than `301`, `302`, `303` or `307`. The second argument of the `return` directive specified the content of the response body:

```
location /disabled {
    default_type text/plain;
    return 200 "OK";
}
```

The preceding configuration will return HTTP status 200 (OK) with the specified response body. To assert correct processing of the body content, we set response content type to `text/plain` using the `default_type` directive.

Access control

Access control restrictions are essential to day-to-day operation. Nginx includes a group of modules that let you allow or deny access depending on various conditions. Nginx denies access to a resource by returning a `403` (Forbidden HTTP) status or 401 (Unauthorized) if accessing the resource requires authentication. This 403 (Forbidden) status code can be intercepted and customized using the `error_page` directive.

Restricting access by IP address

Nginx allows you to permit or deny access to a virtual host or a location by IP address. For that, you can use the directives `allow` and `deny`. They have the following format:

```
allow <IP address> | <IP address>/<prefix size> | all;
deny <IP address> | <IP address>/<prefix size> | all;
```

Specifying an IP address allows or denies access to a single IP address within a location, while specifying an IP address with a prefix size (for example 192.168.0.0/24 or 200.1:980::/32) allows or denies access to a range of IP addresses.

The `allow` and `deny` directives are processed in order of appearance within a location. The remote IP address of a requesting client is matched against the argument of each directive. Once an `allow` directive with a matching address is found, access is immediately allowed. Once a `deny` directive with a matching address is found, access is immediately denied. Once Nginx reaches the `allow` or `deny` directive with the `all` argument, access is immediately allowed or denied, regardless of client's IP address.

This, obviously, allows some variation. Here are some simple examples:

```
server {
    deny 192.168.1.0/24;
    allow all;
    [...]
}
```

The preceding configuration makes Nginx deny access to IP addresses 192.168.1.0 to 192.168.1.255, while allowing access to everyone else. This happens because the `deny` directive is processed first and if matched, is immediately applied. The entire server will be forbidden for specified IP addresses.

```
server {
    [...]
    location /admin {
        allow 10.132.3.0/24;
        deny all;
    }
}
```

The preceding configuration makes Nginx allow access to `location /admin` only to IP addresses in the range 10.132.3.0 to 10.132.3.255. Assuming this range of IP addresses corresponds to some privileged group of users, this configuration makes perfect sense, as only they can access the administrative area of this web application.

Now, we can improve on that and make the configuration more complicated. Assume that more networks need access to this web application's administrative interface, while the IP address 10.132.3.55 needs to be denied access due to technical or administrative reasons. Then, we can extend the preceding configuration as follows:

```
server {
    [...]
    location /admin {
        allow 10.129.1.0/24;
        allow 10.144.25.0/24;
```

```
        deny 10.132.3.55;
        allow 10.132.3.0/24;
        deny all;
    }
}
```

As you can see, the directives `allow` and `deny` are quite intuitive to use. Use them as long as the list of IP addresses to match is not too long. Nginx processes these directives in sequential order, so the time taken to check the client's IP address against the list is on average proportional to the length of the list no matter which directive the address is matched against.

If you need to match client's IP address against a larger list of addresses, consider using the `geo` directive.

Using the geo directive to restrict access by IP address

With the `geo` directive, you can transform an IP address into a literal or numerical value that can later be used to trigger some actions while processing a request.

The `geo` directive has the following format:

```
geo [$<source variable>] $<target variable> { <address mapping> }
```

If the source variable is omitted, the `$remote_addr` variable is used instead. The address mapping is a list of key/value pairs, separated by whitespace. A key is usually an IP address or an IP address with a prefix size specifying a subnet. A value is an arbitrary string of character or a number. Let's look at the following code:

```
geo $admin_access {
    default             deny;
    10.129.1.0/24       allow;
    10.144.25.0/24      allow;
    10.132.3.0/24       allow;
}
```

The value of the source variable is used as a key to look up an entry in the address mapping. Once found, the target variable is assigned to the looked-up value. Otherwise, the default value is used.

With the preceding configuration, the variable `$admin_access` will be assigned the value `allow` if the remote client's IP address originates from the subnet 10.129.1.0/24, 10.144.25.0/24 or 10.132.3.0/24, and `deny` otherwise.

The geo directive builds an efficient succinct data structure to look up the values by IP address in memory. It can handle hundreds of thousands of IP addresses and subnets. To accelerate the startup time, specify IP addresses to the geo directive in ascending order, for example, 1.x.x.x to 10.x.x.x, 1.10.x.x to 1.30.x.x.

The address mapping section can contain directives that affect the behavior of geo address mapping. The following table lists those directives along with their functions:

Directive	Function
default	Specifies a value that is returned when no match is found in the IP address mapping.
proxy	Specifies the address of a proxy server. If a request originates from an address specified by one of the proxy directives, geo will use the last address from the "X-Forwarded-For" header and not from the source variable.
proxy_recursive	If a request originates from an address specified by one of proxy directives, geo will process addresses in the "X-Forwarded-For" header from right-to-left in search of an address outside of the list specified by the proxy directive. In other words, this directive makes geo make a better effort in the search for a real IP address.
ranges	Enables IP address ranges in the mapping list.
delete	Removes the specified sub network from the mapping.

Let's take a look at some examples.

Consider Nginx receives HTTP traffic from an application-level load balancer or an inbound proxy located at IP 10.200.0.1. Since all requests will originate from this IP, we need to examine the "X-Forwarded-For" header in order to obtain the real IP address of the client. We then need to change the preceding configuration as follows:

```
geo $example {
    default                 deny;
    proxy 10.200.0.1;
    10.129.1.0/24       allow;
    10.144.25.0/24      allow;
    10.132.3.0/24       allow;
}
```

If the server is behind a chain of proxies, the real IP address can be obtained by specifying the `proxy_recursive` directive and listing all proxies in the chain:

```
geo $example {
    default                 deny;
    proxy 10.200.0.1;
    proxy 10.200.1.1;
    proxy 10.200.2.1;
    proxy_recursive;
    10.129.1.0/24       allow;
    10.144.25.0/24      allow;
    10.132.3.0/24       allow;
}
```

In the preceding example, proxies have IP addresses 10.200.0.1, 10.200.1.1 and 10.200.2.1. The order the addresses are listed in is not important, as Nginx simply iterates over the addresses specified in the "X-Forwarded-For" header from right-to-left and checks their presence in the `geo` block. The first address outside of the proxy list becomes the real IP address of the client.

If IP addresses need to be specified as ranges instead or in addition to subnets, you can enable this by specifying the `ranges` directive:

```
geo $example {
    default                             deny;
    ranges;
    10.129.1.0-10.129.1.255         allow;
    10.144.25.0-10.144.25.255   allow;
    10.132.3.0/24                           allow;
}
```

Finally, with the help of the `delete` directive, we can define the IP address mapping that allows us to implement an access control procedure analogous to allow and deny directives on a larger scale:

```
geo $admin_access {
    default                 deny;
    10.129.1.0/24       allow;
    10.144.25.0/24      allow;
    10.132.3.0/24       allow;
    delete 10.132.3.55;
}
```

To put this configuration in action, we need to use the `if` section to forbid request those client's IP address do not fall in the `allow` range of the `geo` directive:

```
server {
  [...]
  geo $admin_access {
      default                 deny;
      10.129.1.0/24     allow;
      10.144.25.0/24    allow;
      10.132.3.0/24     allow;
      delete 10.132.3.55;
  }

  location /admin {
      if($admin_access != allow) {
          return 403;
      }
      [...]
  }
}
```

As you can see, the `geo` directive is a powerful and very scalable tool, and access restriction is one of many applications that it can be put to.

Using basic authentication for access restriction

You can configure Nginx to allow access only to those users who can provide the correct combination of a username and a password. Username/password verification is enabled using the `auth_basic` directive:

```
auth_basic <realm name> | off;
```

Realm name specifies the name of a realm (an authenticated area). This argument is usually set to a string that helps users to identify the area they are trying to access (for example *Administrative area, Web mail*, and so on). This string will be passed to the browser and displayed in the username/password entry dialog. In addition to the realm name, you need to specify a file containing a user database using the `auth_basic_user_file` directive:

```
auth_basic_user_file <path to a file>;
```

This file must contain authentication information with a username and a password in each line:

```
username1:encrypted_password1
username2:encrypted_password2
username3:encrypted_password3
username4:encrypted_password4
username5:encrypted_password5
```

This file presumably must be placed outside of document root of any website you are hosting. The access rights must be set up such that Nginx can only read this file, never write or execute.

Passwords must be encrypted using one of the following algorithms:

Algorithms	Comments
CRYPT	Unix DES-based password encryption algorithm
SSHA	Salted Secure Hash Algorithm 1
Deprecated: Do not use	
MD5	Message Digest 5 algorithm
SHA	Unsalted Secure Hash Algorithm 1

The password file can be managed using the `htpasswd` utility from Apache web server. Here are some examples:

Instruction	Command
Create a password file and add user john to the password file	`$ htpasswd -b -d -c /etc/nginx/auth.d/auth.pwd john test`
Add user thomas to the password file	`$ htpasswd -b -d /etc/nginx/auth.d/auth.pwd thomas test`
Replace John's password	`$ htpasswd -b -d /etc/nginx/auth.d/auth.pwd john test`
Remove user john from the password file	`$ htpasswd -D /etc/nginx/auth.d/auth.pwd john`

The option -d forces encryption of passwords using the CRYPT algorithm, which is relatively less secure than SSHA (Salted SHA). To encrypt passwords using SSHA and achieve higher security of your passwords you can use the slappasswd utility from the slapd package:

```
$ sudo apt-get install slapd
$ slappasswd -s test
{SSHA}ZVG7uXWXQVpITwohT0F8yMDGWs0AbYd3
```

Copy the output of slappasswd into the password file. The password file now looks like this:

```
john:{SSHA}ZVG7uXWXQVpITwohT0F8yMDGWs0AbYd3
```

This can be further automated using the echo command:

```
echo "john:"$(slappasswd -s test) > /etc/nginx/auth.d/auth.pwd
```

Once the password file is ready, we can configure password authentication:

```
location /admin {
    auth_basic "Administrative area";
    auth_basic_user_file /etc/nginx/auth.d/auth.pwd;
    [...]
}
```

Password authentication is now enabled; you can navigate to location /admin and see the password prompt:

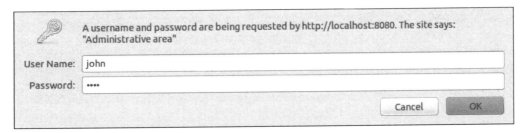

Access to the protected resource will be granted only when a valid combination of username and password is entered into the password prompt.

 Nginx reads and parses the password file every time a request to protected resources is made. This is scalable only when the number of entries in the password file does not exceed a few hundred.

Authenticating users with a subrequest

User authentication can be delegated to another web server using the auth request module. This module must first be enabled at the source code configuration stage using the `-with-http_auth_request_module` command-line switch:

```
$ ./configure -with-http_auth_request_module
$ make
$ make install
```

Now the `auth_request` module is ready to be used. The delegation can be configured as follows:

```
location /example {
    auth_request /auth;
    [...]
}

location = /auth {
    internal;
    proxy_pass http://backend;
    proxy_set_header Content-Length "";
    proxy_pass_request_body off;
}
```

With the preceding configuration, Nginx will execute a subrequest to `location /auth`. This location will pass the subrequest to an external web application (using the `proxy_pass` directive). As the original request might have a request body that the authentication application does not expect, we discard it by specifying `proxy_pass_request_body off` and nullifying the "Content-Length" header using `proxy_set_header`.

In order to reply to a subrequest issued by auth request module, you need to create an application that analyzes data from the original request and replies with HTTP status 401 (Unauthorized) or 403 (Forbidden) in order to block access, and with a successful HTTP status 200 to 299 in order to allow access. Here is an example of such an application in `node.js`:

```
var http         = require('http');
var express      = require('express')
var cookieParser = require('cookie-parser')

var app = express()
```

```
app.use(cookieParser())

app.get('/auth', function(req, res) {
  if(req.cookies.uid) {
    res.sendStatus(200);
  }
  else {
    res.sendStatus(403);
  }
})


app.listen(3000)
```

This application allows access as long a cookie names `uid` is present, and forbids access otherwise.

To run this application, create a directory, create a file named `auth.js` in this directory, and put the preceding source code into this file. After that, install the required modules `express` and `cookie-parser` using npm:

$ npm install express cookie-parser

After that, you can run the application:

$ node auth.js

The application will start listening on port 3000. The following Nginx configuration can be used in order to try the application:

```
location /example {
    auth_request /auth;
}

location = /auth {
    internal;
    proxy_pass http://localhost:3000;
    proxy_set_header Content-Length "";
    proxy_pass_request_body off;
}
```

The subrequest will be delegated to port 3000 of the host, where Nginx is running, and the application will reply to that request.

If the application needs to examine the original request URI, it can be passed using the `proxy_set_header` directive:

```
proxy_set_header X-Auth-URI $request_uri;
```

The original IP address and other original request parameters can be passed to the authenticating application in the same way.

This is how more sophisticated authentication logic can be implemented in Nginx. If you make the application always reply with HTTP status 200, it can be used for purposes other than authentication, such as logging or data injection.

Combining multiple access restriction methods

Multiple access restriction methods can be combined together. For that, they must be both configured and enabled. By default, all configured access restriction methods must be satisfied in order to allow the request. If any of the access restriction methods are not satisfied, Nginx rejects the request with 403 Forbidden HTTP status.

This behavior can be changed using the `satisfy` directive:

```
satisfy all | any;
```

Specifying `satisfy any` in a location makes Nginx accept the request if any of the enabled access restriction methods are satisfied, while specifying `satisfy all` (the default) makes Nginx accept the request only if all enabled access restriction methods are satisfied. To demonstrate how it works, let's extend the preceding example:

```
server {
    [...]
    location /admin {
        auth_basic "Administrative area";
        auth_basic_user_file /etc/nginx/auth.d/admin.users;
        allow 10.132.3.0/24;
        deny all;
        satisfy any;
    }
}
```

This configuration enables and configures both password authentication and IP address restriction. With `satisfy` set to `any`, a user needs to either enter a correct username/password combination or originate from IP address range 10.132.3.0 to 10.132.3.255. This makes users from this network somehow more trusted, as they are not required to enter their username and password in order to access the administrative area.

Summary

In this chapter, you learned how to use the rewrite engine and access control functions. These are essential tools of every web master and site reliability engineer. Excelling in configuring and using these features will help you to solve day-to-day problems more efficiently.

In the next chapter, we will talk about managing inbound and outbound traffic. You will learn how to set various limitations on inbound traffic, how to configure upstream, and how to apply various options to outbound traffic.

5
Managing Inbound and Outbound Traffic

The Internet is an open medium where it is easy and cheap to use someone else's resources. The low cost of usage makes systems vulnerable to intended and unintended abuses and resource usage spikes. The modern Internet is full of dangers such as bots, abusive crawlers, denial of service, and distributed denial of service attacks.

This is where Nginx comes in handy, with a range of features for inbound and outbound traffic management that allows you to stay in control of the quality of your web service.

In this chapter, you will learn:

- How to apply various limitation to inbound traffic
- How to configure upstreams
- How to use various options for outbound connection management

Managing inbound traffic

Nginx has various options for managing inbound traffic. This includes the following:

- Limiting the request rate
- Limiting the number of simultaneous connections
- Limiting the transfer rate of a connection

These features are very useful for managing the quality of your web service and to prevent and mitigate abuses.

Limiting the request rate

Nginx has a built-in module for limiting the request rate. Before you can enable it, you need to configure a shared memory segment (also known as a *zone*) in the `http` section using the `limit_req_zone` directive. This directive has the following format:

```
limit_req_zone <key> zone=<name>:<size> rate=<rate>;
```

The `<key>` argument specifies a single variable or a script (since version 1.7.6) to which the rate limiting state is bound. In simple terms, by specifying the `<key>` argument, you are creating a number of small pipes for each value of the `<key>` argument evaluated at runtime, each of them with its request rate limited with `<rate>`. Each request for a location where this zone is used will be submitted to the corresponding pipe and if the rate limit is reached, the request will be delayed so that the rate limit within the pipe is satisfied.

The `<name>` argument defines the name of the zone and the `<size>` argument defines the size of the zone. Consider the following example:

```
http {
    limit_req_zone $remote_addr zone=rate_limit1:12m rate=30r/m;
    [...]
}
```

In the preceding code, we define a zone named `primary` that is 12 MB in size and has a rate limit of 30 requests per minute (0.5 request per second). We use the `$remote_addr` variable as a key. This variable evaluates into a symbolic value of the IP address the request came from, which can take up to 15 bytes per IPv4 address and even more per IPv6 address.

To conserve space occupied by the key, we can use the variable `$binary_remote_addr` that evaluates into a binary value of the remote IP address:

```
http {
    limit_req_zone $binary_remote_addr zone=rate_limit1:12m
rate=30r/m;
    [...]
}
```

To enable request rate limiting in a location, use the `limit_req` directive:

```
location / {
    limit_req zone=rate_limit1;
}
```

Once a request is routed to `location` /, a rate-limiting state will be retrieved from the specified shared memory segment and Nginx will apply the *Leaky Bucket* algorithm to manage the request rate, as shown in the following figure:

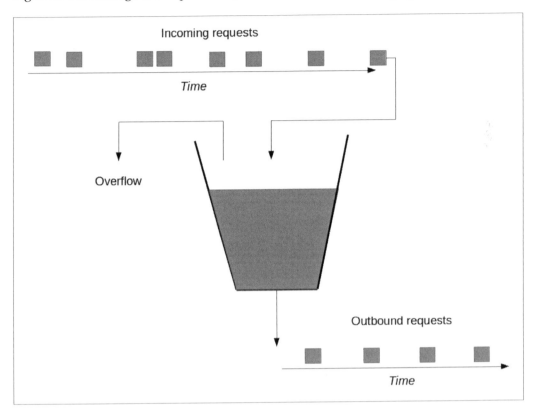

The Leaky Bucket algorithm

According to this algorithm, incoming requests can arrive at an arbitrary rate, but the outbound request rate will never be higher than the specified one. Incoming requests "fill the bucket" and if the "bucket" overflows, excessive requests will get the HTTP status 503 (Service Temporarily Unavailable) response.

Limiting the number of simultaneous connections

Although very practical, request rate limiting cannot help mitigate abuses in case of long-running requests, such as long uploads and downloads.

In this situation, limiting the number of simultaneous connections comes in handy. In particular, it is advantageous to limit the number of simultaneous connections from a single IP address.

Enabling the simultaneous connections limit starts from configuring a shared memory segment (a zone) for storing state information, just like when limiting the request rate. This is done in the `http` section using the `limit_conn_zone` directive. This directive is similar to the `limit_req_zone` directive and has the following format:

```
limit_conn_zone <key> zone=<name>:<size>;
```

In the preceding command, the `<key>` argument specifies a single variable or a script (since version 1.7.6) to which the connection limiting state is bound. The `<name>` argument defines the name of the zone and the `<size>` argument defines the size of the zone. Consider the following example:

```
http {
    limit_conn_zone $remote_addr zone=conn_limit1:12m;
    [...]
}
```

To conserve the space occupied by the key, we can again use the variable `$binary_remote_addr`. It evaluates into a binary value of the remote IP address:

```
http {
    limit_conn_zone $binary_remote_addr zone=conn_limit1:12m;
    [...]
}
```

To enable simultaneous connection limiting in a location, use the `limit_conn` directive:

```
location /download {
    limit_conn conn_limit1 5;
}
```

The first argument of the `limit_conn` directive specifies the zone used to store connection limiting state information, and the second argument is the maximum number of simultaneous connections.

For each connection with an active request routed to `location /download`, the `<key>` argument is evaluated. If the number of simultaneous connections sharing the same value of the key surpasses 5, the server will reply with HTTP status 503 (Service Temporarily Unavailable).

 Note that the size of the shared memory segment that the `limit_conn_ zone` directive allocates is fixed. When the allocated shared memory segment gets filled, Nginx returns HTTP status 503 (Service Temporarily Unavailable). Therefore, you have to adjust the size of the shared memory segment to account for the potential inbound traffic of your server.

Limiting the transfer rate of a connection

The transfer rate of a connection can also be limited. Nginx has a number of options for this purpose. The `limit_rate` directive limits the transfer rate of a connection in a location to the value specified in the first argument:

```
location /download {
    limit_rate 100k;
}
```

The preceding configuration will limit the download rate of any request for `location /download` to 100 KBps. The rate limit is set per request. Therefore, if a client opens multiple connections, the total download rate will be higher.

Setting the rate limit to 0 switches off transfer rate limiting. This is helpful when a certain location needs to be excluded from the rate limit restriction:

```
server {
    [...]
    limit_rate 1m;

    location /fast {
        limit_rate 0;
    }
}
```

The preceding configuration limits the transfer rate of each request to a given virtual host to 1 MBps, except for `location /fast`, where the rate is unlimited.

The transfer rate can also be limited by setting the value of the variable
`$limit_rate`. This option can be elegantly used when rate-limiting needs
to be enabled upon a particular condition:

```
if ($slow) {
    set $limit_rate 100k;
}
```

There is also an option to postpone the rate restriction until a certain amount of data
has been transferred. This can be achieved by using the `limit_rate_after` directive:

```
location /media {
    limit_rate 100k;
    limit_rate_after 1m;
}
```

The preceding configuration will enforce the rate limit only after the first megabyte
of request data has been sent. Such behavior is useful, for example, when streaming
video, as the initial part of the stream is usually prebuffered by the video player.
Returning the initial part faster improves video startup time without clogging the
disk I/O bandwidth of the server.

Applying multiple limitations

The limitations described in the previous section can be combined to produce more
sophisticated traffic management strategies. For example, you can create two zones
for limiting the number of simultaneous connections with different variables and
apply multiple limits at once:

```
http {
    limit_conn_zone $binary_remote_addr zone=conn_limit1:12m;
    limit_conn_zone $server_name zone=conn_limit2:24m;
    [...]
    server {
        [...]
        location /download {
            limit_conn conn_limit1 5;
            limit_conn conn_limit2 200;
        }
    }
}
```

The preceding configuration will limit the number of simultaneous connections per
IP address to five; at the same time the total number of simultaneous connections per
virtual host will not exceed 200.

Managing outbound traffic

Nginx also has a variety of options for outbound traffic management:

- Distributing outbound connections among multiple servers
- Configuring backup servers
- Enabling persistent connections with backend servers
- Limiting transfer rate while reading from backend servers

To enable most of these functions, the first thing you need is to declare your upstream servers explicitly.

Declaring upstream servers

Nginx allows you to declare upstream servers explicitly. You can then refer to them multiple times as a single entity from any part of the http configuration. If the location of your server or servers changes, there is no need to go over the entire configuration and adjust it. If new servers join a group, or existing servers leave a group, it's only necessary to adjust the declaration and not the usage.

An upstream server is declared in the upstream section:

```
http {
    upstream backend  {
        server server1.example.com;
        server server2.example.com;
        server server3.example.com;
    }
    [...]
}
```

The upstream section can only be specified inside the http section. The preceding configuration declares a logical upstream named backend with three physical servers. Each server is specified using the server directive. The server directive has the following syntax:

```
server <address> [<parameters>];
```

The <address> parameter specifies an IP address or a domain name of a physical server. If a domain name is specified, it is resolved at the startup time and the resolved IP address is used as the address of a physical server. If the domain name resolves into multiple IP addresses, a separate entry is created for each of the resolved IP addresses. This is equivalent to specifying a server directive for each of these addresses.

The address can contain optional port specification, for example, `server1.example.com:8080`. If this specification is omitted, port 80 is used. Let's look at an example of upstream declaration:

```
upstream numeric-and-symbolic  {
    server server.example.com:8080;
    server 127.0.0.1;
}
```

The preceding configuration declares an upstream named `numeric-and-symbolic`. The first server in the server list has a symbolic name and its port changed to `8080`. The second server has the numerical address `127.0.0.1` that corresponds to the local host and the port is `80`.

Let's look at another example:

```
upstream numeric-only  {
    server 192.168.1.1;
    server 192.168.1.2;
    server 192.168.1.3;
}
```

The preceding configuration declares an upstream named `numeric-only`, which consists of three servers with three different numerical IP addresses listening on the default port.

Consider the following example:

```
upstream same-host  {
    server 127.0.0.1:8080;
    server 127.0.0.1:8081;
}
```

The preceding configuration declares an upstream named `same-host`, which consists of two servers with the same address (`127.0.0.1`) that listen on different ports.

Let's look at the following example:

```
upstream single-server  {
    server 192.168.0.1;
}
```

The preceding configuration declares an upstream named `single-server`, which consists of only one server.

The following table lists the optional parameters of the `server` directive and their description:

Syntax	Description
weight=<number>	This specifies the numerical weight of the server. It is used for distributing connections among the servers. The default value is 1.
max_ fails=<number>	This specifies the maximum number of connection attempts after which the server is considered as unavailable. The default value is 1.
fail_ timeout=<number>	This specifies the time after which a failing server will be marked as unavailable. The default value is 10 seconds.
backup	This labels a server as a backup server.
down	This labels a server as unavailable.
max_ conns=<number>	This limits the number of simultaneous connections to the server.
resolve	This instructs Nginx to automatically update the P addresses of a server specified using a symbolic name and apply these addresses without restarting Nginx.

Using upstream servers

Once an upstream server is declared, it can be used in the `proxy_pass` directive:

```
http {
    upstream my-cluster  {
        server server1.example.com;
        server server2.example.com;
        server server3.example.com;
    }
    [...]
    server {
        [...]
        location @proxy {
            proxy_pass http://my-cluster;
        }
    }
}
```

The upstream can be referred multiple times from the configuration. With the preceding configuration, once the location @proxy is requested, Nginx will pass the request to one of the servers in the server list of the upstream.

The algorithm for resolving the final address of an upstream server is shown in the following figure:

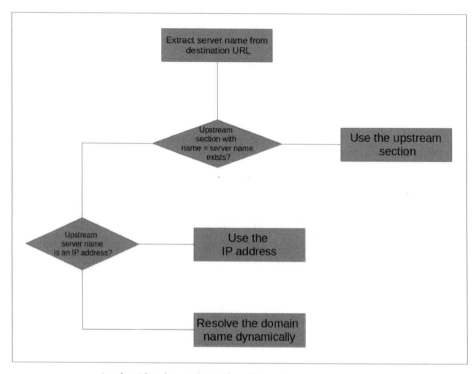

An algorithm for resolving the address of an upstream server

Because a destination URL can contain variables, it is evaluated at runtime and parsed as HTTP URL. The server name is extracted from the evaluated destination URL. Nginx looks up an upstream section that matches the server name and if such exists, forwards the request to one of the servers from the upstream server list according to a request distribution strategy.

If an upstream section that matches the server name exists, Nginx checks if the server name is an IP address. If so, Nginx uses the IP address as the final address of the upstream server. If the server name is symbolic, Nginx resolves the server name in DNS into an IP address. If successful, the resolved IP address is used as the final address of the upstream server.

The address of the DNS server or servers can be configured using the `resolver` directive:

```
resolver 127.0.0.1;
```

The preceding directive takes a list of IP addresses of the DNS servers as its arguments. If a server name cannot be successfully resolved using the configured resolver, Nginx returns HTTP status 502 (Bad Gateway).

When an upstream contains more than one server in the server list, Nginx distributes requests among these servers in an attempt to split the load among the available servers. This is also called clustering, as multiple servers act as one—altogether they are called a cluster.

Choosing a request distribution strategy

By default, Nginx uses Round-robin algorithm while distributing requests among available upstream servers, as shown in the following figure:

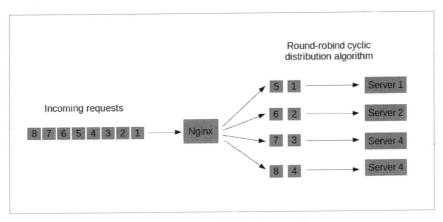

Round-robin cyclic distribution algorithm

According to this algorithm, incoming requests are assigned to servers from the upstream server list in equal proportions and cyclic order. This ensures equal distribution of incoming requests among available servers, but does not ensure equal distribution of the load among servers.

If servers in the upstream server list have varying capacities, the distribution algorithm can be changed to account for that. This is what the parameter `weight` is used for. This parameter specifies the relative weight of a server in comparison to other servers. Consider an installation where one of the servers is twice as capable as the other two. We can configure Nginx for this installation as follows:

```
upstream my-cluster  {
    server server1.example.com weight=2;
    server server2.example.com;
    server server3.example.com;
}
```

The first server is configured to have twice as high a weight as the other servers and the request distribution strategy changes accordingly. This is shown in the following figure:

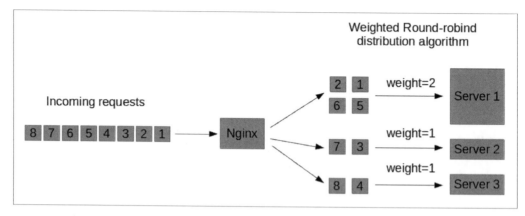

Weighted round-robin

In the preceding figure, we can see that two out of four incoming requests will go to server 1, one will go to server 2, and another one will be going to server 3.

The round-robin strategy does not guarantee that requests from the same client will be always forwarded to the same server. The latter might be a challenge for web applications that expect the same client to be served by the same server or at least need some affinity of users to servers to perform efficiently.

With Nginx, you can solve this by using the IP hash request distribution strategy. With the IP hash distribution strategy, each request from a given IP address will be forwarded to the same backend server. This is achieved by hashing the client's IP address and using the numerical value of the hash to choose the server from the upstream server list. To enable the IP hash request distribution strategy, use the `ip_hash` directive in the upstream section:

```
upstream my-cluster  {
    ip_hash;
    server server1.example.com;
    server server2.example.com;
    server server3.example.com;
}
```

The preceding configuration declares an upstream with three underlying servers and enables the IP hash request distribution strategy for each of them. A request from a remote client will be forwarded to one of the servers from this list and it is always the same for all requests from the client.

If you add or remove a server from the list, the correspondence between IP addresses and servers will change and your web application will have to deal with this situation. To make this problem somehow easier to handle, you can mark a server as unavailable using the down parameter. Requests to this server will be forwarded to the next available server:

```
upstream my-cluster   {
    ip_hash;
    server server1.example.com;
    server server2.example.com down;
    server server3.example.com;
}
```

The preceding configuration declares the server2.example.com server unavailable and once a request is targeted to this server, the next available server will be chosen (server1.example.com or server3.example.com).

If an IP address is not a convenient input for the hash function, you can use the hash directive instead of ip_hash to choose an input that is more convenient. The only argument of this directive is a script, which is evaluated at runtime and produces a value used as the input for the hash function. This script can contain, for example, a cookie, an HTTP header, a combination of an IP address and a user agent, an IP address and a proxied IP address, and so on. Take a look at the following example:

```
upstream my-cluster   {
    hash "$cookie_uid";
    server server1.example.com;
    server server2.example.com;
    server server3.example.com;
}
```

The preceding configuration uses a cookie named uid as input for the hash function. If the cookie stores a unique ID of a user, each user's requests will be forwarded to a fixed server in the upstream server list. If a user does not have a cookie yet, the variable $cookie_uid evaluates to an empty string and produces a fixed hash value. Therefore, all requests from users without the uid cookie are forwarded to a fixed server from the preceding list.

In the next example, we will use a combination of a remote IP address and the user agent field as input for the hash function:

```
upstream my-cluster   {
    hash "$remore_addr$http_user_agent";
    server server1.example.com;
    server server2.example.com;
    server server3.example.com;
}
```

The preceding configuration relies on the diversity of user agent field and prevents a concentration of users from proxied IP addresses on a single server.

Configuring backup servers

Some servers in the server list can be marked as *backup*. By doing so, you tell Nginx that these servers should not be normally used and used only when all non-backup servers do not respond.

To illustrate the use of backup servers, imagine that you run a **Content Distribution Network (CDN)** where a number of geographically distributed edge servers handle user traffic and a set of centralized content servers generate and distribute content to the edge servers. This is shown in the following figure.

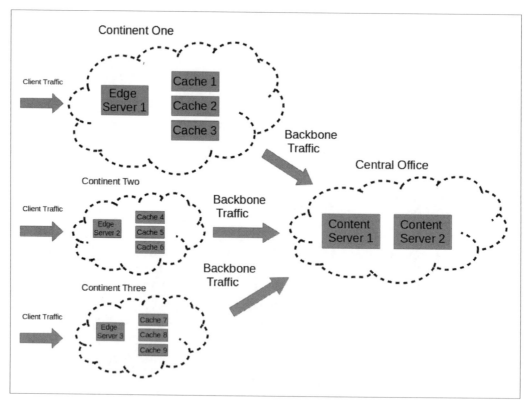

A Content Distribution Network

The edge servers are co-located with a set of highly-available caches that do not alter the content obtained from the content servers, but simply store it. The caches have to be used as long as any of them is available.

However, when none of the caches are available for some reason, the edge server can contact the content servers—although it is not desirable. Such behavior (called degradation) can remedy the situation until the outage of caches is resolved, while keeping the service available.

Then, the upstream on the edge server can be configured as follows:

```
upstream my-cache  {
    server cache1.mycdn.com;
    server cache2.mycdn.com;
    server cache3.mycdn.com;

    server content1.mycdn.com backup;
    server content2.mycdn.com backup;
}
```

The preceding configuration declares the servers `cache1.mycdn.com`, `cache2.mycdn.com` and `cache3.mycdn.com` as primary servers to contact. They will be used as long as any of them is available.

We then list the `content1.mycdn.com` and `content2.mycdn.com` servers as backup by specifying the `backup` parameter. These servers will be contacted only if none of the primary servers are available. This feature of Nginx provides flexibility in the way the availability of your system is managed.

Determining whether a server is available

How do you define that a server is available? For most applications, connectivity errors are hard signs of an unavailable server, but what if an error is software generated? It might be worth trying the next server if a server is available on the transport layer (over TCP/IP) but returns HTTP errors such as `500` (Internal Server Error) and `503` (Service Unavailable) or even softer errors such as `403` (Forbidden) or `404` (Not found). If the upstream server is a proxy itself, it might be necessary to handle HTTP errors `502` (Bad Gateway) and `504` (Gateway Timeout).

Nginx allows you to specify availability and retrial conditions using the directives `proxy_next_upstream`, `fastcgi_next_upstream`, `uwsgi_next_upstream`, `scgi_next_upstream`, and `memcached_next_upstream`. Each of these directives receives a list of conditions that will be treated as errors while communicating with an upstream server, and make Nginx retry with another server. In addition to that, if the number of unsuccessful interaction attempts with a server is larger than the value of the `max_fails` parameter for the server (the default value is `1`), the server will be marked as unavailable for a period specified by the `fail_timeout` directive (the default value is `10` seconds).

The following table lists all possible values for the arguments of the directives `proxy_next_upstream`, `fastcgi_next_upstream`, `uwsgi_next_upstream`, `scgi_next_upstream`, and `memcached_next_upstream`:

Value	Meaning
error	A connection error has occurred or an error during sending a request or receiving a reply has occurred
timeout	A connection timed out during setup, sending a request or receiving a reply
invalid_header	The upstream server has returned an empty or invalid reply
http_500	The upstream server returned a reply with HTTP status code 500 (Internal Server Error)
http_502	The upstream server returned a reply with HTTP status code 502 (Bad Gateway)
http_503	The upstream server returned a reply with HTTP status code 503 (Service Unavailable)
http_504	The upstream server returned a reply with HTTP status code 504 (Gateway Timeout)
http_403	The upstream server returned a reply with HTTP status code 403 (Forbidden)
http_404	The upstream server returned a reply with HTTP status code 404 (Not Found)
off	Disables passing requests to the next server

The default value for the preceding directives is `error timeout`. This makes Nginx retry a request with another server only if a connectivity error or a timeout has occurred.

Here is an example of a configuration that uses the `proxy_next_upstream` directive:

```
location @proxy {
    proxy_pass http://backend;
    proxy_next_upstream error timeout http_500 http_502 http_503
http_504;
}
```

The preceding configuration extends the default retrial and availability option and enables retrying with the next server in case of connectivity error, upstream error (502, 503, or 504) or a connection timeout.

Enabling persistent connections

By default, Nginx does not keep connections with upstream servers open. Keeping the connections open can significantly improve the performance of your system. This is because persistent connections eliminate the connection setup overhead every time a request is made to a given upstream server.

To enable persistent connections for an upstream, use the keepalive directive in the upstream section:

```
upstream my-cluster  {
    keepalive 5;
    server server1.example.com;
    server server2.example.com;
    server server3.example.com;
}
```

The only argument of the keepalive directive specifies the minimum number of inactive persistent connections in the connection pool of this upstream. If the number of inactive persistent connections grows beyond this number, Nginx closes as many connections as needed to stay within this number. This guarantees that a specified number of hot and ready-to-go connections are always available for use. At the same time, these connections consume the resources of backend servers, so this number must be chosen cautiously.

To use persistent connections with HTTP proxying, further tweaks are required:

```
location @proxy {
    proxy_pass http://backend;
    proxy_http_version 1.1;
    proxy_set_header Connection "";
}
```

In the preceding configuration, we change the HTTP version to 1.1 so that persistent connections are expected by default. We also clear the Connection header so that the Connection header from the original request does not influence the proxied request.

Limiting the transfer rate of an upstream connection

The transfer rate of a connection with an upstream can be limited. This feature can be used to reduce stress on the upstream server. The `proxy_limit_rate` directive limits the transfer rate of an upstream connection in a location to the value specified in the first argument:

```
location @proxy {
    proxy_pass http://backend;
    proxy_buffering on;
    proxy_limit_rate 200k;
}
```

The preceding configuration will limit the rate of connections with the specified backend to 200 KBps. The rate limit is set per request. If Nginx opens multiple connections to the upstream server, the total rate will be higher.

> Rate limiting works only if proxy response buffering is switched on using the `proxy_buffering` directive.

Summary

In this chapter, you learned about a number of tools for inbound and outbound traffic management. These tools will help you to ensure the reliability of your web service and implement complex caching schemes.

In the next chapter, you'll learn how to squeeze the most performance out of your web server and optimize resource usage—performance tuning.

6
Performance Tuning

Performance tuning is the improvement of system performance. In our context, it is the performance of an entire web service or an individual web server. The need for such activity arises when there is a real or anticipated performance problem, such as excessive response latency, insufficient upload or download rate, lack of system scalability, or excessive use of computer system resources for seemingly low service usage.

In this chapter, we will look at a number of topics that deal with performance problems using features of Nginx. Each section explains when and how a solution is applicable; that is, what kind of performance problems it addresses.

In this chapter you will learn about:

- How to optimize static file retrieval
- How to set up response compression
- How to optimize data buffer allocation
- How to accelerate SSL by enabling session caching
- How to optimize worker process allocation on multi-core systems

Optimizing static file retrieval

Static file retrieval performance directly affects visitors' perceived website performance. This happens because web pages usually contain numerous references to dependent resources. These resources need to be quickly retrieved before the entire page can be rendered. The faster the web server can start returning a static file (lower latency) and the higher the parallelism of retrieval, the higher the perceived performance of the website.

When the latency is the driving factor, it is important that files are returned predominantly from the main memory, as it has much lower latency compared to hard drives.

Fortunately, the operating system already takes very good care of that through filesystem cache. You only need to stimulate cache usage by specifying some advisory parameters and eliminating waste:

```
location /css {
    sendfile on;
    sendfile_max_chunk 1M;
    [...]
}
```

By default, Nginx reads the content of a file into the user space before sending to the client. This is suboptimal and can be avoided by using the sendfile() system call if it is available. The sendfile() function implements a zero-copy transfer strategy by copying data from one file descriptor to another bypassing user space.

We enable sendfile() by specifying the sendfile on parameter in code. We limit the maximum amount of data that sendfile() can send in one invocation to 1 MB using the sendfile_max_chunk directive. In this way, we prevent a single fast connection from occupying the whole worker process.

 Response body filters such as the .gzip compressor require response data in the user space. They cannot be combined with a zero-copy strategy and consequently with sendfile(). When enabled, they cancel the effect of sendfile().

The preceding configuration is optimized for latency. Compare it to the example from the *Setting up Nginx to serve static data* section in *Chapter 2, Managing Nginx*. You will see that the tcp_nopush directive is gone. The off state of this option will make network utilization a bit less efficient, but will deliver data—including the HTTP header—to the client as soon as possible.

With tcp_nopush set to on, the first packet of the response will be sent as soon as the chunk of data is obtained by sendfile().

Another aspect of static file retrieval is large file download. In this case, the startup time is not as important as the download throughput or, in other words, the download speed that a server can attain while returning a large file. Caching stops being desirable for large files. Nginx reads them sequentially, so cache hits are much less likely for them. Cached segments of a large file would therefore simply pollute the cache.

On Linux, caching can be bypassed by using Direct I/O. With Direct I/O enabled, the operating system translates read offsets into the underlying block device addresses, and queues read requests directly into the underlying block device queue. The following configuration shows how to enable Direct I/O:

```
location /media {
    sendfile off;
    directio 4k;
    output_buffers 1 256k;
    [...]
}
```

The `directio` directive takes a single argument that specifies the minimum size a file must have in order to be read with Direct I/O. In addition to specifying `direction`, we extend the output buffer using the `output_buffers` directive in order to increase system call efficiency.

Note that Direct I/O blocks the worker processes during reads. This reduces parallelism and throughput of file retrieval. To avoid blocking and increase parallelism, you can enable **Asynchronous I/O (AIO)**:

```
location /media {
    sendfile off;
    aio on;
    directio 4k;
    output_buffers 1 256k;
    [...]
}
```

On Linux, AIO is available as of kernel version 2.6.22 and it is non-blocking only in combination with Direct I/O. AIO and Direct I/O can be combined with `sendfile()`:

```
location /media {
    sendfile on;
    aio on;
    directio 4k;
    output_buffers 1 256k;
    [...]
}
```

In this case, files smaller than the size specified in `directio` will be send using `sendfile()`, or else with AIO plus Direct I/O.

As of Nginx version 1.7.11, you can delegate file read operations to a pool of threads. This makes perfect sense if you are not limited by memory or CPU resources. As threads do not require Direct I/O, enabling them on large files will lead to aggressive caching:

```
location /media {
    sendfile on;
    aio threads;
    [...]
}
```

Threads are not compiled by default (at the moment of writing this chapter), so you have to enable them using the with-threads configuration switch. In addition to that, threads can work only with epoll, kqueue, and eventport event processing methods.

With threads, both higher parallelism and caching can be attained without blocking the worker process, although threads and communication between threads require some additional resources.

Enabling response compression

Performance of your website can be improved by enabling response compression using GZIP. Compression reduces the size of a response body, reduces the bandwidth required to transfer the response data, and ultimately makes sure the resources of your website are delivered to the client side sooner.

Compression can be enabled using the gzip directive:

```
location / {
    gzip on;
    [...]
}
```

This directive is valid in the http, server, location, and if sections. Specifying off as the first argument of this directive disables compression in the corresponding location if it was enabled in outer sections.

By default, only documents with MIME type *text/HTML* are compressed. To enable compression for other types of documents, use the `gzip_types` directive:

```
location / {
    gzip on;
    gzip_types
text/html text/plain text/css application/x-javascript text/xml
    application/xml application/xml+rss text/javascript;
    [...]
}
```

The preceding configuration enables compression for MIME types that hypertext documents, cascading style sheets, and JavaScript files appear to be in. These are the types of documents that benefit most from the compression, as text files and source code files — if they are large enough — usually contain a lot of entropy.

Archives, images, and movies are not suitable for compression, as they are usually already compressed. Executable files are less suitable for compression, but can benefit from it in some cases.

It makes sense to disable compression for small documents, as compression efficiency might not be worth the efforts — or even worse — might be negative. In Nginx, you can implement compression using the `gzip_min_length` directive. This directive specifies the minimum length a document must be in order to be eligible for compression:

```
location / {
    gzip on;
    gzip_min_length 512;
    [...]
}
```

With the preceding configuration, all documents smaller than 512 bytes will not be compressed. The length information that is used to apply this restriction is extracted from the Content-Length response header. If no such header is present, the response will be compressed regardless of its length.

Response compression comes at a cost: it is CPU-intensive. You need to consider that in your capacity planning and system design. If CPU utilization becomes a bottleneck, try reducing the compression level using the `gzip_comp_level` directive.

The following table lists some other directives that affect the behavior of compression:

Directive	Function
gzip_disable <regex>	If the User-Agent field of a request matches the specified regular expression, the compression for that request will be disabled.
gzip_comp_level <level>	This specifies the GZIP compression level to use. The lowest is 1 and the highest is 9. These values correspond to options -1 ... -9 of the gzip command.

The preceding directives can help you fine-tune the response compression in your system.

The efficiency of response body compression can be monitored via the $gzip_ratio variable. This variable indicates the attained compression ratio equal to the ratio of the size of the original response body to the size of the compressed one.

The value of this variable can be written to the log file and later extracted and picked up by your monitoring system. Consider the following example:

```
http {
    log_format gzip
'$remote_addr - $remote_user [$time_local] $status '
        '"$request" $body_bytes_sent "$http_referer" '
        '"$http_user_agent" "$host" $gzip_ratio';

    server {
        [...]
        access_log  /var/log/nginx/access_log gzip;
        [...]
    }
}
```

The preceding configuration creates a log file format named gzip and uses this format to log HTTP requests in one of the virtual hosts. The last field in the log file will indicate the attained compression ratio.

Optimizing buffer allocation

Nginx uses buffers to store request and response data at various stages. Optimal buffer allocation can help you spare memory consumption and reduce CPU usage. The following table lists directives that control buffer allocation and the stages they are applied to:

Directive	Function
`client_body_buffer_size <size>`	This specifies the size of the buffer that is used to receive the request body from the client.
`output_buffers <number> <size>`	This specifies the number and the size of buffers that are used to send the response body to the client in case no acceleration is used.
`gzip_buffers <number> <size>`	This specifies the number and the size of the buffers that are used to compress the response body.
`proxy_buffers <number> <size>`	This specifies the number and the size of the buffers that are used to receive the response body from a proxied server. This directive makes sense only if buffering is enabled.
`fastcgi_buffers <number> <size>`	This specifies the number and the size of the buffers that are used to receive the response body from a FastCGI server.
`uwcgi_buffers <number> <size>`	This specifies the number and the size of the buffers that are used to receive the response body from a UWCGI server.
`scgi_buffers <number> <size>`	This specifies the number and the size of the buffers that are used to receive the response body from a SCGI server.

As you can see, most of the directives take two arguments: a number and a size. The number argument specifies the maximum number of buffers that can be allocated per request. The size argument specifies the size of each buffer.

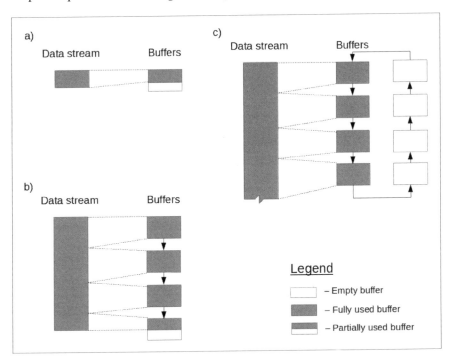

The preceding figure illustrates how buffers are allocated for a data stream. Part **a** shows what happens when an input data stream is shorter than the buffer size specified in the directives above. The data stream occupies the entire buffer even though the space for the whole buffer is allocated from the heap. Part **b** shows a data stream that is longer than a single buffer, but shorter than the longest allowed chain of buffers. As you can see, if the buffers are used in the most efficient way, some of them will be fully used and the last one might be only partially used. Part **c** shows a data stream that is much longer than the longest chain of buffers allowed. Nginx tries to fill all available buffers with input data and flushes them once the data is sent. After that, empty buffers wait until more input data becomes available.

New buffers are allocated as long as there are no free buffers at hand and input data is available. Once the maximum number of buffers is allocated, Nginx waits until used buffers are emptied and reuses them. This makes sure that no matter how long the data stream, it will not consume more memory per request (the number of buffers multiplied by the size) than specified by the corresponding directive.

The smaller the buffers, the higher the allocation overhead. Nginx needs to spend more CPU cycles to allocate and free buffers. The larger the buffers, the larger memory consumption overhead. If a response occupies only a fraction of a buffer, the remainder of the buffer is not used—even though the entire buffer has to be allocated from the heap.

The minimum portion of the configuration that the buffer size directives can be applied to is a location. This means that if mixtures of large and small responses share the same location, the combined buffer usage pattern will vary.

Static files are read into buffers controlled by the `output_buffers` directive unless `sendfile` is set to on. For static files, multiple output buffers don't make much sense, as they are filled in the blocking mode anyway (this means a buffer cannot be emptied while the other one is being filled). However, larger buffers lead to lower system call rate. Consider the following example:

```
location /media {
    output_buffers 1 256k;
    [...]
}
```

If the output buffer size is too large without threads or AIO, it can lead to long blocking reads that will affect worker process responsiveness.

When a response body is pipelined from a proxied server, FastCGI, UWCGI, or SCGI server, Nginx is able to read data into one part of the buffers and simultaneously send the other part to the client. This makes the most sense for long replies.

Assume you tuned your TCP stack before reading this chapter. The total size of a buffer chain is then connected to the kernel socket's read and write buffer sizes. On Linux, the maximum size of a kernel socket read buffer can be examined using the following command:

```
$ cat /proc/sys/net/core/rmem_max
```

While the maximum size of a kernel socket write buffer can be examined using the following command:

```
$ cat /proc/sys/net/core/wmem_max
```

These settings can be changed using the `sysctl` command or via `/etc/sysctl.conf` at system startup.

In my case, both of them are set to `163840` (160 KB). This is low for a real system, but let's use it as an example. This number is the maximum amount of data Nginx can read from or write to a socket in one system call without the socket being suspended. With reads and writes going asynchronously, we need a buffer space no less than the sum of `rmem_max` and `wmem_max` for optimal system call rate.

Assume that the preceding Nginx proxies long files with `rmem_max` and `wmem_max` settings. The following configuration must yield the lowest system call rate with the minimum amount of memory per request in the most extreme case:

```
location @proxy {
    proxy_pass http://backend;
    proxy_buffers 8 40k;
}
```

The same considerations apply to the `fastcgi_buffers`, `uwcgi_buffers`, and `scgi_buffers` directives.

For short response bodies, the buffer size has to be a bit larger than the predominant size of a response. In this case, all replies will fit into one buffer—only one allocation per request will be needed.

For the preceding setup, assume that most of the replies fit 128 KB, while some span up to dozens of megabytes. The optimal buffer configuration will be somewhere between `proxy_buffers 2 160k` and `proxy_buffers 4 80k`.

In the case of response body compression, the size of the GZIP buffer chain must be downscaled by the average compression ratio. For the preceding setup, assume that the average compression ratio is 3.4. The following configuration must yield the lowest system call rate with a minimal amount of memory per request in presence of response body compression:

```
location @proxy {
    proxy_pass http://backend;
    proxy_buffers 8 40k;
    gzip on;
    gzip_buffers 4 25k;
}
```

In the preceding configuration we make sure that in the most extreme case, if half of the proxy buffers are being used for reception, the other half is ready for compression. GZIP buffers are configured in a way that makes sure that the compressor output for half of the uncompressed data occupies half of the output buffers, while the other half of the buffers with compressed data are sent to the client.

Enabling SSL session reuse

An SSL session is started by a handshake procedure that involves multiple round trips (see the following figure). The client and server have to exchange four messages with a latency of around 50 milliseconds each. In total, we have at least 200 milliseconds of overhead while establishing a secure connection. In addition to that, both the client and the server need to perform public-key cryptographic operations in order to share a common secret. These operations are computationally expensive.

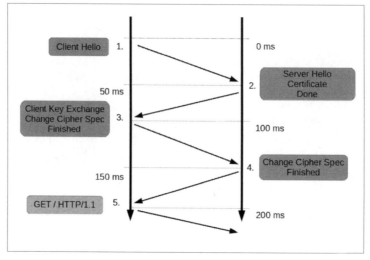

Normal SSL handshake

The client can request an abbreviated handshake in effect (see the following figure), saving a full round-trip of 100 milliseconds and avoiding the most expensive part of the full SSL handshake:

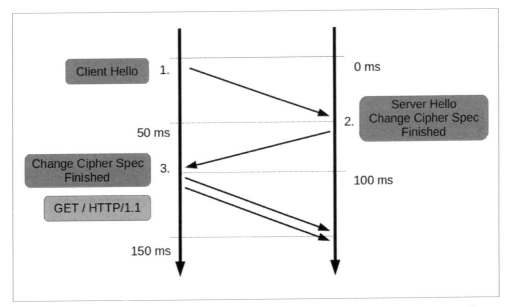

Abbreviated handshake

The abbreviated handshake can be accomplished either through the *session identifiers* mechanism defined by RFC 5246, or through the *session tickets* mechanism detailed in RFC 5077.

To make abbreviated handshakes with session identifiers possible, the server needs to store session parameters in a cache keyed by a session identifier. In Nginx, this cache can be configured to be shared with all worker processes. When a client requests an abbreviated handshake, it provides the server with a session identifier so that it can retrieve session parameters from the cache. After that, the handshake procedure can be shortened and public-key cryptography can be skipped.

To enable SSL session cache, use the `ssl_session_cache` directive:

```
http {
    ssl_session_cache builtin:40000;
    [...]
}
```

This configuration enables SSL session caching with built-in OpenSSL session cache. The number in the first argument (40000) specifies the size of the cache in sessions. The built-in cache cannot be shared between worker processes. Consequently, this reduces efficiency of SSL session reuse.

The following configuration enables SSL session caching with a cache shared between worker processes:

```
http {
    ssl_session_cache shared:ssl:1024k;
    [...]
}
```

This creates a shared SSL session cache named `ssl` and enables SSL session reuse with this cache. The size of the cache is now specified in bytes. Each session occupies around 300 bytes in such cache.

It is possible to perform an abbreviated SSL handshake without the server state using an SSL session tickets mechanism. This is done by packaging session parameters into a binary object and encrypting it with a key known only to the server. This encrypted object is called a session ticket.

A session ticket then can be safely transferred to the client. When the client wishes to resume a session, it presents the session ticket to the server. The server decrypts it and extracts the session parameters.

Session tickets are an extension of the TLS protocol and can be used with TLS 1.0 and further (SSL is a predecessor of TLS).

To enable session tickets, use the `ssl_session_tickets` directive:

```
http {
    ssl_session_tickets on;
    [...]
}
```

Naturally, both mechanisms can be enabled at once:

```
http {
    ssl_session_cache shared:ssl:1024k;
    ssl_session_tickets on;
    [...]
}
```

For security reasons, cached session lifetime is limited so that session parameters cannot be attacked while session is active. Nginx sets the default maximum SSL session lifetime to 5 minutes. If security is not a big concern and visitors spend considerable time on your website, you can extend the maximum session lifetime, increasing the efficiency of SSL in effect.

The maximum SSL session lifetime is controlled by the `ssl_session_timeout` directive:

```
http {
    ssl_session_cache shared:ssl:1024k;
    ssl_session_tickets on;
    ssl_session_timeout 1h;
    [...]
}
```

The preceding configuration enables both session reuse mechanisms and sets the maximum SSL session lifetime to 1 hour.

Worker processes allocation on multi-core systems

If your Nginx workload is CPU-bound, such as when using response compression on proxied content, on systems with multiple processors or multiple processor cores, it might be possible to obtain additional performance by associating each worker process with its own processor/core.

In a multi-core processor, each core has its own instance of **Translation Lookaside Buffer (TLB)** that is used by the memory-management unit to accelerate virtual address translation. In a preemptive multitasking operating system, each process has its own virtual memory context. When an operating system assigns an active process to a processor core and the virtual memory context does not match the context that filled the TLB of that processor core, the operating system has to flush the TLB as its content is no longer valid.

The new active process then receives a performance penalty, because it has to fill the TLB with new entries as it reads or writes memory locations.

Nginx has an option to "stick" a process to a processor core. On a system with a single Nginx instance, worker processes will be scheduled most of the time. In such circumstances, there is a very high probability that the virtual memory context does not need to be switched and TLB does not need to be flushed. The "stickiness" of a process then becomes useful. The "stickiness" is called CPU affinity.

Consider a system with four processor cores. The CPU affinity can be configured as follows:

```
worker_processes 4;
worker_cpu_affinity 0001 0010 0100 1000;
```

This configuration assigns each worker to its own processor core. The configuration directive `worker_cpu_affinity` receives many arguments as many worker process are to be started. Each argument specifies a mask, where a bit with a value of 1 specifies affinity with the corresponding processor, and a bit with a value of 0 specifies no affinity with the corresponding processor.

> CPU affinity does not guarantee an increase in performance, but make sure to give it a try if your Nginx server is performing CPU-bound tasks.

Summary

In this chapter, you learned a number of recipes that will help you tackle performance and scalability challenges of your system. It is important to remember that these recipes are not solutions for all possible performance problems and represent mere trade-offs between different ways of using the resources of your system.

Nevertheless, they are must-haves in the toolbox of a web master or a site reliability engineer who wants to master Nginx and its performance and scalability features.

Index

A

access control
about 80
access, restricting by IP address 80, 81
basic authentication, using for access
restriction 85-87
geo directive used, for restricting access by
IP address 82-85
multiple access restriction methods,
combining 90
users, authenticating with
subrequest 88, 89
algorithms, for password encryption
CRYPT 86
MD5 86
SHA 86
SSHA 86
Asynchronous I/O (AIO) 113

B

binary
creating, with debugging information 50
binary expression 16
binary operators
!= 16
!~ 16
!~* 16
= 16
~ 16
~* 16
break flag 72
buffer allocation
optimizing 116-120

C

cache loader process 62
cache manager 63
caching
about 61
border cases, handling 68, 69
cache availability, improving 66, 67
cache efficiency, improving 66
cache key, selecting 64, 65
caches, configuring 61-63
enabling 63, 64
exceptions, handling 68, 69
upstream response header 63
captures 77
Certificate Signing Request (CSR) 44
clustered setup 27
command, identification data
Common name (CN) 45
Country name (C) 44
Locality or city (L) 44
Organizational Unit (OU) 45
Organization (O) 45
State or province (S) 44
commands, CentOS version
defining 4
configuration directives
client_body_temp_path 47
fastcgi_temp_path 47
proxy_temp_path 47
scgi_temp_path 47
uwsgi_temp_path 47
Content Distribution Network (CDN) 106

M

master process
about 26
defining 26
multi-core systems
worker processes allocation,
    used on 123, 124

N

Nginx
about 1, 35
building 6
configuration best practices 22
configuration settings' inheritance
    rules 18-20
configuring 9
connection processing architecture 26-28
http section 13
if section 15-17
inclusions 12
installing 1
installing, from source files 4
installing, on CentOS/Scientific Linux 3, 4
installing, on Red Hat Enterprise Linux 3, 4
installing, on Ubuntu 2
issues 29
limit_except section 18
location section 14
other section types 18
sample configuration 21, 22
sections 13
server section 13
setting up, to serve static data 42, 43
solutions 29
starting 28, 29
stopping 28, 29
troubleshooting 7
upstream section 14
URL 1
value types 10
variables 10, 11
Nginx, as reverse proxy
about 51, 52
backend configuration, right way 53, 54

cookies, handling 57
downloads, accelerating 61
errors, handling 59, 60
outbound IP address, selecting 60
redirects, handling 55, 56
setting up 52, 53
SSL, using 58, 59
transparency, adding 54, 55
Nginx configuration
URL 22
Nginx files
locations 6
Nginx installation
structure 8
Nginx, on Ubuntu
alternatives 2
Nginx source files
downloading 5
troubleshooting 5
URL 5

O

outbound traffic, managing
about 99
backup servers, configuring 106, 107
persistent connections, enabling 109
request distribution strategy,
    selecting 103-105
server availability, determining 107, 108
transfer rate of upstream connection,
    limiting 110
upstream servers, declaring 99, 100
upstream servers, using 101, 102

P

parameter files, Nginx configuration folder
fastcgi_params 8
koi-utf 8
koi-win 8
mime.types 8
naxsi.rules (optional) 8
proxy_params 8
scgi_params 8
uwsgi_params 8
win-utf 8

U

Ubuntu
  Nginx, installing 2
unary expression 16
unary operators
  -d 16
  !-d 16
  -e 16
  !-e 16

  -f 16
  !-f 16
  -x 16
  !-x 16

W

worker processes
  about 26
  allocating 40-42
  allocating, on multi-core systems 123, 124

Thank you for buying
Nginx Essentials

About Packt Publishing

Packt, pronounced 'packed', published its first book, *Mastering phpMyAdmin for Effective MySQL Management*, in April 2004, and subsequently continued to specialize in publishing highly focused books on specific technologies and solutions.

Our books and publications share the experiences of your fellow IT professionals in adapting and customizing today's systems, applications, and frameworks. Our solution-based books give you the knowledge and power to customize the software and technologies you're using to get the job done. Packt books are more specific and less general than the IT books you have seen in the past. Our unique business model allows us to bring you more focused information, giving you more of what you need to know, and less of what you don't.

Packt is a modern yet unique publishing company that focuses on producing quality, cutting-edge books for communities of developers, administrators, and newbies alike. For more information, please visit our website at www.packtpub.com.

About Packt Open Source

In 2010, Packt launched two new brands, Packt Open Source and Packt Enterprise, in order to continue its focus on specialization. This book is part of the Packt Open Source brand, home to books published on software built around open source licenses, and offering information to anybody from advanced developers to budding web designers. The Open Source brand also runs Packt's Open Source Royalty Scheme, by which Packt gives a royalty to each open source project about whose software a book is sold.

Writing for Packt

We welcome all inquiries from people who are interested in authoring. Book proposals should be sent to author@packtpub.com. If your book idea is still at an early stage and you would like to discuss it first before writing a formal book proposal, then please contact us; one of our commissioning editors will get in touch with you.

We're not just looking for published authors; if you have strong technical skills but no writing experience, our experienced editors can help you develop a writing career, or simply get some additional reward for your expertise.

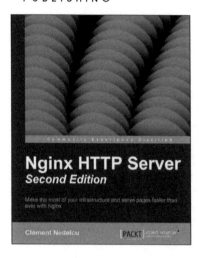

Nginx HTTP Server

Second Edition

ISBN: 978-1-78216-232-2   Paperback: 318 pages

Make the most of your infrastructure and serve pages faster than ever with Nginx

1. Complete configuration directive and module reference.

2. Discover possible interactions between Nginx and Apache to get the best of both worlds.

3. Learn to configure your servers and virtual hosts efficiently.

4. A step-by-step guide to switching from Apache to Nginx.

Mastering NGINX

ISBN: 978-1-84951-744-7   Paperback: 322 pages

An in-depth guide to configuring NGINX for any situation, including numerous examples and reference tables describing each directive

1. An in-depth configuration guide to help you understand how to best configure NGINX for any situation.

2. Includes useful code samples to help you integrate NGINX into your application architecture.

3. Full of example configuration snippets, best-practice descriptions, and reference tables for each directive.

Please check **www.PacktPub.com** for information on our titles

Nginx Module Extension

ISBN: 978-1-78216-304-6   Paperback: 128 pages

Customize and regulate the robust Nginx web server, and write your own Nginx modules efficiently

1. Install Nginx from its source on multiple platforms.

2. Become acquainted with core Nginx modules and their configuration options.

3. Explore optional and third party module extensions along with configuration directives.

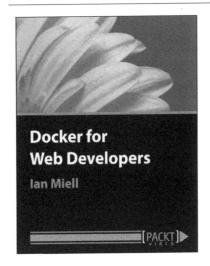

Docker for Web Developers [Video]

ISBN: 978-1-78439-067-9   Duration: 01:31 hours

Accelerate your web development skills on real web projects in record time with Docker

1. Supercharge your web development process while ensuring that everything works smoothly.

2. Win at 2048 using Docker's commit and restore functionality.

3. Use the Docker Hub workflow to automate the rebuilding of your web projects.

4. Full of realistic examples, this is a step-by-step journey to becoming a Docker expert!.

Please check **www.PacktPub.com** for information on our titles

Made in the USA
Middletown, DE
27 January 2016